4

ENGLISH IN ACTION

THIRD EDITION

NATIONAL GEOGRAPHIC
LEARNING

BARBARA H. FOLEY
ELIZABETH R. NEBLETT

Australia · Brazil · Mexico · Singapore · United Kingdom · United States

National Geographic Learning,
a Cengage Company

English in Action Level 4 Third Edition
Barbara H. Foley, Elizabeth R. Neblett

Publisher: Sherrise Roehr

Executive Editor: Sarah Kenney

Managing Development Editor:
Claudienma Mimó

Senior Development Editor:
Lewis Thompson

Associate Development Editor: Katie Davis

Assistant Editor: Becky Long

Media Researcher: Leila Hishmeh

Director of Global Marketing: Ian Martin

Product Marketing Manager: Dalia Bravo

Sr. Director, ELT & World Languages:
Michael Burggren

Production Manager: Daisy Sosa

Content Project Manager: Beth Houston

Manufacturing Customer Account Manager:
Mary Beth Hennebury

Composition: MPS North America LLC

Cover/Text Design: Lisa Trager

Art Director: Brenda Carmichael

Cover Image: ©Jim Nix/Getty Images

For permission to use material from this text or product, submit all requests online at **cengage.com/permissions**
Further permissions questions can be emailed to
permissionrequest@cengage.com

Student Edition:
ISBN: 978-1-337-90597-8

Student Edition + OWB:
ISBN: 978-1-337-90688-3

National Geographic Learning
20 Channel Center Street
Boston, MA 02210
USA

Locate your local office at **international.cengage.com/region**

Visit National Geographic Learning online at **NGL.Cengage.com/ELT**
Visit our corporate website at **www.cengage.com**

Printed in Mexico
Print Number: 02 Print Year: 2022

ACKNOWLEDGMENTS

The authors and publisher would like to thank the following reviewers and advisory panel members:

Karin Abell
Durham Technical Community College, Durham, NC

Angela Addy
Passaic County Community College, Passaic, NJ

Beth Anglin
Bucks County Community College, Newtown, PA

Irma Baack
Harper College, Schaumburg, IL

Teresita Bautista
Paramount Adult Education, CA

Rod Bennett
Emily Griffith Technical College, Denver, CO

Anne Bertin
Union County College, New Jersey

Patricia Bone
Montgomery College, Rockville, MD

Carlo Buzzi
North Shore Community College, Danvers, MA

Julia Cantu
MiraCosta College, Oceanside, CA

Fang Chen
Central New Mexico Community College, Albuquerque, NM

Kathryn Clark
Daytona State College, Daytona Beach, FL

Lin Cui
William Rainey Harper College, Palatine, IL

Andre DeSandies
Union County College, New Jersey

Lois Eisenber
Bucks County Community College, Newtown, PA

Linda Foster
Hillsborough County, FL

Tracy Fung
Palomar College, San Marcos, CA

Litsa Georgiou
Union County College, New Jersey

Deborah Greene
Sharon Technical College, Hollywood, FL

Jill Harold
University of North Texas, Denton, TX

Harriet Hirschfeld
Bucks County Community College, Newtown, PA

Kathleen Hiscock
Portland Adult Education, Portland, ME

Lorraine Hromalik
Bowers/Whitley Adult Community School, Tampa, FL

Liz Hughes
Rosie's Place, Boston, MA

Dawn Humphry
University of Arkansas Cossatot Community College, Nashville, AR

Kim Johnson
Palomar College, San Marcos, CA

Christopher Kilmer
Emily Griffith Technical College, Denver, CO

Eileen Krai
Bucks County Community College, Newtown, PA

Caron Lieber
Palomar College, Fallbrook, CA

Mayra Lopez
MiraCosta College, Oceanside, CA

Melissa Lutz
University of Arkansas Cossatot Community College, De Queen, AR

Diann Mandile
Emily Griffith Technical College, Denver, CO

Cheo Massion
College of Marin, Kentfield, CA

Lynn Meng
Union County College, New Jersey

Gregor Mieder
Metropolitan State University, Denver, CO

Susan Moser
Portland Community College, Portland, OR

Susana Murillo
Palomar College, San Marcos, CA

Karen Nelson
Pittsburg State University, Pittsburg, KA

Sergei Paromchik
Hillsborough County Public Schools, Tampa, FL

Claudia Pena
Houston Community College, Houston, TX

Dinah Perren
Palomar College, Oceanside, CA

Kandyce Pinckney
Emily Griffith Technical College, Denver, CO

Howard Pomann
Union County College, New Jersey

Nicole Powell
SUNY Orange, Bloomingburg, NY

Tami Richey
Palomar College, San Marcos, CA

Julie Roberts
Georgia Piedmont Technical College, Doravilla, GA

Christi Stilley
CARIBE Refugee Program, Tampa, FL

Gail Voorhes
Palomar College, Ramona, CA

Huaxin Xu
Union County College, New Jersey

Rochelle Yanike-Hale
Portland Adult Education, Portland, ME

Beth Zarret
Bucks County Community College, Newtown, PA

Miriam Zemen
Montgomery College, Silver Spring, MD

CONTENTS

CONTENTS

Contents **vii**

UNIT 1 EDUCATION

AT WORK Discuss work schedules, daily habits, and being late

ACADEMIC Collect and record information from classmates; identify and recall key facts; scan a text for important information; illustrate statements with examples; check texts for grammar and formatting

CIVICS Identify different types of courses and services available at a college or university; complete a sample college application

Students study in the 180-seat Grand Reading Room, part of the Joe and Rika Mansueto Library at the University of Chicago.

A Look at the pictures and answer the questions.

a.

c.

b.

d.

1. Which classroom is most similar to a high school classroom in your native country?

2. Which classroom is similar to your current classroom?

3. Which classroom has the most students?

4. Which classroom has the fewest students?

5. Which classroom looks the most casual?

6. Which classroom looks the most formal?

B Work in groups. Discuss typical classrooms in your native countries. Ask and answer the questions.

1. How many students are in a classroom?

2. Do students wear uniforms?

3. How do students sit? Do they sit in rows, in groups, or in a circle?

4. What does the teacher usually do?

5. What objects do students often use in the classroom?

C **ACADEMIC** **LET'S TALK.** Work in groups. Ask and answer questions about your current school and complete the chart. Then, discuss two more places in your school.

A: Does our school have a director's office?

B: Yes, it does.

C: Where is it?

D: It's on the first floor, near the entrance.

Place	Does our school have _____?	Where is it?
1. a director's or principal's office		
2. a teachers' room		
3. a bookstore		
4. a library		
5. a counselor's office		
6. a learning center or tutoring center		
7. a computer lab		
8. a cafeteria		
9. restrooms		
10. a gym		
11. a student center		
12. a study room		
13. a dormitory		
14. a copy room for students		
15.		
16.		

I You We They	study do not study don't study	English.
He She	studies does not study doesn't study	
It	works. does not work. doesn't work.	

The simple present can be used to describe everyday activities, habits, and repeated actions.

A Circle the correct forms of the verbs to make true statements about high school in your native country.

1. The school year **begins / doesn't begin** in September.
2. The school day **starts / doesn't start** at 8:30 a.m.
3. Classes **meet / don't meet** on Saturdays.
4. High school students **choose / don't choose** some of their own courses.
5. Students **write / don't write** their papers on a computer.
6. Students **study / don't study** with students of the same ability.
7. Most students **work / don't work** after school.
8. Students **wear / don't wear** uniforms.

B Complete the sentences about high school in your native country. Use the correct forms of the verbs.

1. Teachers (move) _____ *move / do not move /don't move* _____ from classroom to classroom.
2. Students (call) _____ their teachers by their first names.
3. Teachers (wear) _____ jeans in class.
4. Teachers (sit) _____ on their desks during class.
5. There (be) _____ after-school programs for students.
6. Families (pay) _____ for textbooks.
7. The teachers (give) _____ many tests.
8. There (be) _____ homework every night.

C **LET'S TALK.** Work in groups. Read the statements in Exercise B. Discuss your answers.

Do	I you we they	**walk** to school? **study** in the library? **work**?
Does	he she	

Yes, you **do**. Yes, I **do**. Yes, we **do**. Yes, they **do**. Yes, he **does**. Yes, she **does**.

No, you **don't**. No, I **don't**. No, we **don't**. No, they **don't**. No, he **doesn't**. No, she **doesn't**.

More information in Appendix A.

A Listen to Sophie and Lizzy, two college roommates. Complete the questions with *Do* or *Does*. Then, answer the questions. 🎧2

1. ___Does___ Sophie take all of her courses in the morning?   _____Yes, she does._____
2. _____ you take your English class in the morning?   _____
3. _____ Sophie keep her side of the room neat?   _____
4. _____ Sophie get up early?   _____
5. _____ you get up early?   _____
6. _____ Sophie study in the room?   _____
7. _____ you study in your bedroom?   _____
8. _____ Lizzy and Sophie have the same schedule?   _____
9. _____ Lizzy keep her side of the room neat?   _____
10. _____ you keep your home neat?   _____
11. _____ Lizzy hand in all her papers on time?   _____
12. _____ you hand in your homework on time?   _____

B **LET'S TALK.** Work in groups. Are you more like Sophie or Lizzy? Explain why.

ACTIVE GRAMMAR   Simple Present: *Wh-* Questions

What Where When Why How How often	do does	I you we they he she	study?

Who	**studies** English? **goes** to work? **lives** nearby?

More information in Appendix A.

Who takes a singular verb when it asks about the subject.
Who **speaks** English?
When *who* asks about the object, the verb can be singular or plural.
Who **do** you **visit**?
Who **does** she **call**?

A **ACADEMIC** **LET'S TALK.** Work in small groups. Interview each other about your daily schedules and habits. Then, write one more question to ask your group.

Questions	You	Partner 1	Partner 2
1. What time do you get up?			
2. What time do you leave for school?			
3. How do you get to school?			
4. How long does it take to get to school?			
5. When do you do your homework?			
6.			

B **Pronunciation: Linking:** *do you* Listen and repeat. 🎧3

1. What do you do?
2. Where do you work?
3. How do you get home?
4. Where do you live?
5. Why do you study here?
6. What do you do on weekends?

C **AT WORK** Answer these questions about your classmates' habits and schedules.

1. Who always arrives on time?
2. Who usually takes the bus?
3. Who often arrives late?
4. Who goes to work after class?
5. Who usually asks questions in class?
6. Who works on the weekends?

D Write three more questions using *who*. Then, ask a classmate your questions.

Present Continuous: Statements

I	am			
You We They	are	(not)	using a computer. studying for a test. sitting on a chair.
He She	is		

The present continuous is often used to talk about an action that is happening now.
    She **is texting** her friend.
The present continuous can also describe a temporary action.
    They **are living** in an apartment for now.
    (Meaning: They expect to move soon.)

A LET'S TALK. Work in groups. Write two sentences about each photo using the present continuous. Make one of the sentences for each photo negative.

1.

a. *The students are not working in groups.*

b. _____

3.

a. _____

b. _____

2.

a. _____

b. _____

4.

a. _____

b. _____

ACTIVE GRAMMAR / Present Continuous: Questions

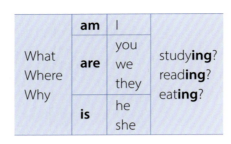

Am	I		
Are	you we they	working?	
Is	he she		

	am	I	
What Where Why	**are**	you we they	studying? reading? eating?
	is	he she	

Who	**is**	studying? cooking?

More information in Appendix A.

A LET'S TALK. Work with a partner. Answer the questions about your class.

1. Are the students taking a test?
2. Are they working together?
3. Are they speaking English?
4. Is the teacher helping the students?

5. Is anyone using a dictionary?
6. Are the students writing?
7. Are the students drinking water?
8. Is the teacher writing on the board?

B Look around your classroom. Write answers to the questions.

1. Who is sitting next to the door? _____
2. Who is talking to the teacher? _____
3. Who is speaking another language? _____
4. What is the teacher doing? _____
5. Where are you sitting? _____
6. What are you wearing? _____

C Listen and write the questions you hear. Then, answer the questions. Your teacher will refer to Appendix D.

1. _Are any students eating?_ _____
2. _____
3. _____
4. _____
5. _____
6. _____

appear	have	miss	smell
believe	hear	need	sound
belong	know	own	taste
feel	like	prefer	understand
hate	look	see	want

Non-action verbs are usually used in the simple present, not the present continuous. Non-action verbs often show feelings, senses, thoughts, or possession.

He **knows** my name.

I **miss** my grandparents.

There are some exceptions, because some verbs can show both action and non-action.

I**'m having** a cup of tea.

How **are** you **feeling**?

They**'re seeing** a movie.

A Look at the picture and write sentences in your notebook. Use the words below and the simple present or present continuous.

1. Students / like / to meet / the student center
   Students like to meet at the student center.
2. They / need to relax / between classes
3. Lee and Jamal / play / chess
4. Some students / study / together
5. Some music / play / in the background
6. Students / hope to pass / their exams
7. They / (not) feel / stressed
8. Lana and her boyfriend / watch / TV
9. Bill / look / bored
10. He / (not) like / reality shows
11. Two students / buy / pizza
12. The pizza / smell / good

A **ACADEMIC** Listen to the description of the University of Texas at San Antonio. Circle the correct answers and complete the notes. 🎧4

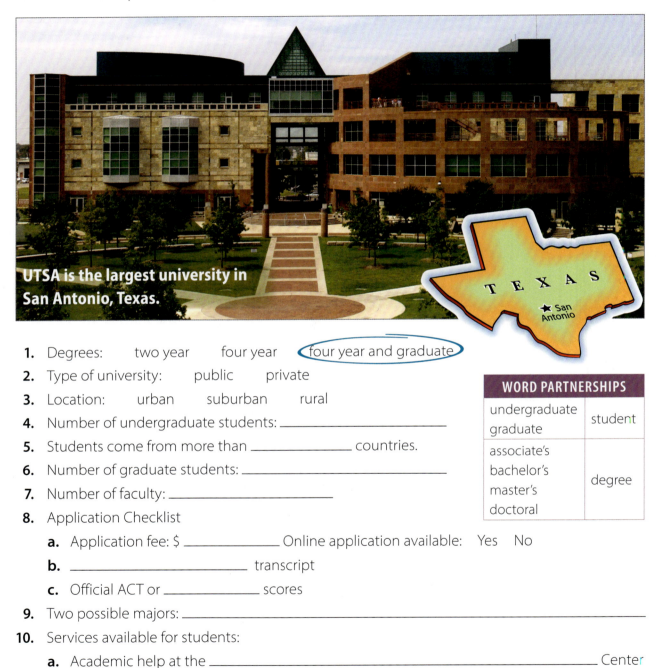

UTSA is the largest university in San Antonio, Texas.

TEXAS
★ San Antonio

1. Degrees: two year   four year   (four year and graduate)
2. Type of university: public   private
3. Location: urban   suburban   rural
4. Number of undergraduate students: _____
5. Students come from more than _____ countries.
6. Number of graduate students: _____
7. Number of faculty: _____
8. Application Checklist

   a. Application fee: $ _____ Online application available: Yes   No

   b. _____ transcript

   c. Official ACT or _____ scores

9. Two possible majors: _____

10. Services available for students:

    a. Academic help at the _____ Center

    b. A health clinic and _____ counseling

    c. Examples of student activities: _____

    d. Orientation for _____ and _____

WORD PARTNERSHIPS	
undergraduate graduate	student
associate's bachelor's master's doctoral	degree

B **ACADEMIC** Circle *True* or *False*.

1. The University of Texas at San Antonio (UTSA) is a large university. (True) False
2. UTSA is a private university. True False
3. UTSA has a graduate school. True False
4. The university has three campuses. True False
5. The main campus is downtown. True False
6. UTSA employs about eight hundred faculty. True False
7. Students pay $60 for the application fee. True False
8. Families attend orientation with their children. True False

C Listen and write short answers to the questions about the University of Texas at San Antonio. 🎧5

1. _____ No, it isn't. _____
2. _____
3. _____
4. _____
5. _____
6. _____
7. _____
8. _____

D Complete the sentences with the simple present form of the verb.

1. The University of Texas (have) _____ has _____ many campuses.

2. Over 26,000 undergraduate students (study) _____ at UTSA.

3. Future students (pay) _____ an application fee.

4. A student (take) _____ standardized tests before he or she goes to UTSA.

5. The Learning Center (have) _____ tutors and counselors for the students.

6. Many students (play) _____ in music groups and (participate)

   _____ in international student organizations.

7. The university (give) _____ the students free career counseling.

8. Students (go) _____ to the employment service when they (need)

   _____ to find jobs.

New Jersey Institute of Technology (NJIT)

New Jersey Institute of Technology (NJIT) is located in Newark, New Jersey, ten miles from New York City. It is a four-year public research university focused on the fields of science, technology, engineering, and math, as well as architecture, design, and management. NJIT offers both bachelor's and graduate degrees.[1] More than 90 percent of its students come from New Jersey. The average age of entering students is 18.

In addition to an application, students who are interested in applying to NJIT need to prepare the following materials for admission:

- the application fee; in 2018, the fee was $75
- an official high school transcript of grades
- official SAT (Scholastic Aptitude Test) or ACT (American College Testing) scores; The average SAT score is 1218 and average ACT score is 26.
- For non-US citizens, students must send photocopies of visas or permanent resident cards.

The university requires interested students to have a strong math and science background. Students normally have at least a 3.0 GPA (Grade Point Average), four years of high school English, and two years of science, including one of a laboratory science such as chemistry.

NJIT gives students the option of distance learning, allowing them to take some of their classes online. NJIT also offers many master's degree programs and graduate certificates fully online. Online courses are designed for students who need flexibility.

In addition, NJIT offers many evening and early morning classes. It also has summer and winter sessions. Students who need extra preparation get special instruction, English as a second language classes, or tutoring. Like many other colleges today, NJIT requires that each student have a computer. The university offers good deals for students who need to buy computers and necessary software.

There are dormitories for students who prefer to live on campus or who live too far away to commute. Students can participate in many clubs, sports teams, and organizations. For example, NJIT has a radio station and a video game club.

If you think you might be interested in NJIT, look at its website, njit.edu, for more information. 🎧6

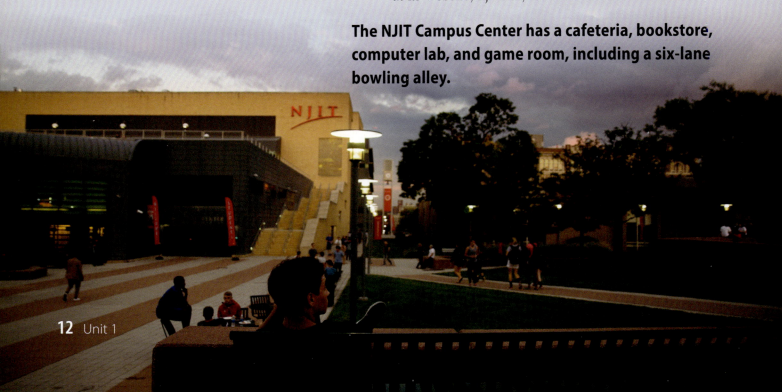

The NJIT Campus Center has a cafeteria, bookstore, computer lab, and game room, including a six-lane bowling alley.

A **ACADEMIC** Scan the text to find the answers to the questions.

1. Where is the school located?
2. Does NJIT have graduate programs?
3. How much was the application fee in 2018?
4. What is the average SAT score for NJIT students?
5. What is the grade point average of most NJIT students?
6. Can students get graduate degrees online?

B **CIVICS** Read the text. Then, underline and number the answers to the questions in the text.

1. What percentage of the students come from New Jersey?
2. Does the college accept foreign students?
3. What is *distance learning*?
4. Who takes online courses?
5. Does NJIT have classes in the summer?
6. What kinds of services are available for students who need more preparation?
7. What kinds of clubs and organizations can students join?

C Go online. Research a college or university that interests you. Report three or more facts that you find.

There are more than 60 research centers and laboratories at NJIT.

A Read.

Indent the first line of each paragraph. Use the tab key on your computer.

Type your name and the date.

Amelia Mendez
September 25

My Schedule — Write a title

    I am a student at Union County College. The school is in New Jersey. This is my first semester, and my major is education.

    I have a busy schedule. On Mondays and Wednesdays, I have an ESL grammar and listening class from 5:00 p.m. to 7:30 p.m. I have a reading and writing course on Tuesdays and Thursdays from 6:30 p.m. to 9:00 p.m. On Fridays, I have a math class from 6:00 p.m to 8:30 p.m.

    I belong to a study group, and we study together for three hours on Saturday mornings. I do my homework at home after my classes. I spend about two hours a night on my homework. Math is my hardest subject.

    I like my classes and my school. I have a lot of friends. I like spending time at the student center.

B Write about your school schedule and classes. Answer the questions.

1. What school do you attend? Where is it located?
2. What is your weekly school schedule?
3. Are your classes difficult, easy, or just right?
4. How often do you have tests?
5. When and where do you study? How many hours do you study a week?
6. Do you like your school? Why?

C **ACADEMIC** Read a classmate's text. Answer the questions.

1. How many paragraphs are there? Did your partner indent the first line of each paragraph?
2. Is your partner's name and the date at the top of the page?
3. What is the title of your partner's text? _____

Such as

Such as can be used to introduce examples.

> Lisa likes many of her classes, **such as** art history and English literature.

D `ACADEMIC` Complete each sentence with appropriate examples. Then, write two more sentences using *such as*.

1. My classmates come from different countries, such as _____ and _____ .

2. In our English class, we are studying many things, such as _____ and _____ .

3. Computers are useful for many things, such as _____ and _____ .

4. A medical student has to study sciences, such as _____ and _____ .

5. Languages such as _____ and _____ are difficult to learn.

6. Sports such as _____ and _____ are very popular in the United States.

7. _____

   _____

8. _____

   _____

E `ACADEMIC` There is one underlined verb mistake in each sentence. Correct the mistakes.

1. The Division of Physical Education <u>offer</u> *offers* many recreational programs.

2. NJIT <u>is develop</u> many programs to attract women and minority students to engineering and the sciences.

3. UTSA's campuses <u>provides</u> opportunities for many students.

4. Some students <u>are preferring</u> to study from their own homes, using computers.

5. What kind of exams <u>students usually take</u>?

6. My roommate <u>is belonging</u> to the women's volleyball team.

7. This test <u>is looking</u> difficult.

A **CIVICS** Imagine that you are applying to college. Complete the sample college application.

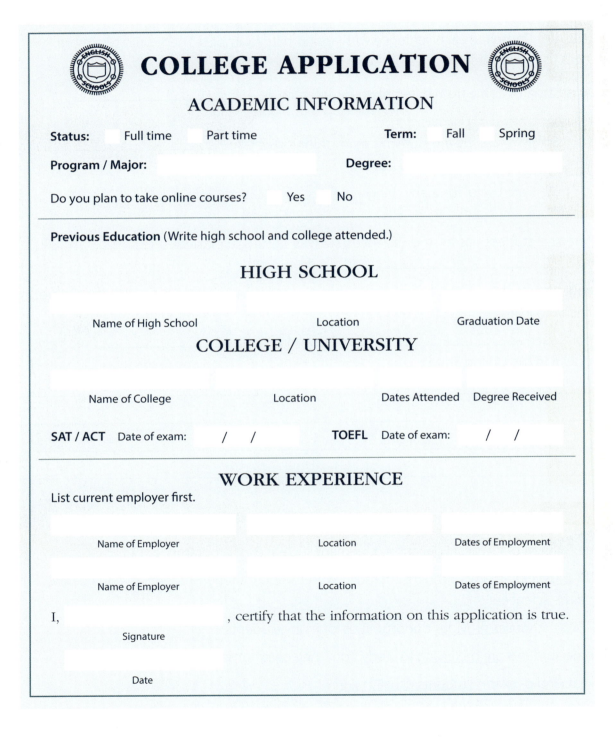

COLLEGE APPLICATION

ACADEMIC INFORMATION

Status: ☐ Full time ☐ Part time   **Term:** ☐ Fall ☐ Spring

Program / Major: _____   **Degree:** _____

Do you plan to take online courses? ☐ Yes ☐ No

Previous Education (Write high school and college attended.)

HIGH SCHOOL

_____

Name of High School   Location   Graduation Date

COLLEGE / UNIVERSITY

_____

Name of College   Location   Dates Attended   Degree Received

SAT / ACT   Date of exam: ___/___/___   **TOEFL**   Date of exam: ___/___/___

WORK EXPERIENCE

List current employer first.

_____

Name of Employer   Location   Dates of Employment

_____

Name of Employer   Location   Dates of Employment

I, _____, certify that the information on this application is true.

Signature

_____

Date

COLONIAL TIMES

A man in colonial-style clothing teaches tourists about US history in Boston, Massachusetts.

AT WORK Ask and answer questions about work history; prepare for and give a presentation

ACADEMIC Take notes on information you hear; ask and answer questions about key information from a text; infer the meaning of new vocabulary; brainstorm before writing

CIVICS Identify and recall key information about people and events in US history; compare facts about life today and in colonial times

A **CIVICS** Read. Then, look at the map of the original 13 colonies and discuss the questions.

> A **colony** is a group of people who are living in a new land, but the government of their home country is still in charge. A **colony** can also be the new land in which these people live.
> The King of England was the ruler of the 13 **colonies**.

THE 13 COLONIES 1775

1. Is your state one of the original 13 colonies of the United States?

2. Which colony was the farthest south?

3. Which colony was the farthest north?

4. Which state is Plymouth in?

5. Which state is Jamestown in?

6. What year is this map from?

A   Write the simple past forms of the verbs.

Regular verbs

1. call _____called_____
2. cook _____
3. need _____
4. play _____

5. talk _____
6. use _____
7. travel _____
8. watch _____

I You We They He She It	**moved** **didn't move**	to Canada.

Irregular verbs

1. buy _____
2. drive _____
3. go _____

4. grow _____
5. make _____
6. read _____

7. sleep _____
8. write _____
9. get _____

See the chart of irregular verbs in Appendix A.

B   Look at the pictures and listen to the comparisons between life today and life in colonial times. Number the pictures in the order you hear them discussed. 🎧7

C   Work with a partner. Look at each picture and describe life in Colonial America.

D Complete the sentences about life in Colonial America. Write the verbs from the box in the simple past. Some of the verbs are negative. You can use some words more than once.

buy	get	grow	play	sleep	travel	watch
cook	~~go~~	have	read	talk	use	write

1. People _____ *didn't go* _____ to supermarkets. They _____ their own food.

2. People _____ over open fires. They _____ stoves.

3. People _____ milk from their cows. They _____ milk at the supermarket.

4. Families _____ candles for light.

5. People _____ on mattresses with box springs.

6. At night, families _____ TV. They _____ books and _____ games.

7. People _____ to one another on cellphones. They _____ letters to one another.

8. People _____ by horse and wagon. They _____ cars.

Faneuil Hall in Boston, MA, 1700s

Faneuil Hall today

E Complete the sentences to compare the activities you usually do now to the things you did when you were a child.

Now,

1. I _____ every day.

2. I _____ on the weekends.

3. _____ .

When I was a child,

4. I _____ every day.

5. I _____ on the weekends.

6. _____ .

| I He She It | was
was not
wasn't | young. |
| You We They | were
were not
weren't | young. |

There	was	a garden.
	was not wasn't	a refrigerator.
	were	few schools.
	were not weren't	large schools.

A Complete the sentences with *was*, *wasn't*, *were*, or *weren't*.

1. Life _____ *wasn't* _____ easy for the first colonists.

2. The first homes _____ small buildings made of wood and mud.

3. There _____ a refrigerator in the kitchen.

4. There _____ bathrooms, either. There _____ a small outhouse in the backyard.

5. Windows _____ small.

6. At first, there _____ only a few schools in the colonies.

7. There _____ any telephones to communicate.

8. By 1776, the population of the colonies _____ about two and a half million.

B 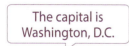 **LET'S TALK.** Use the information below to read about life today and talk about life in 1790. Use the simple past.

> The capital is Washington, D.C.

> The capital was New York City.

Today

1. The capital is Washington, D.C.
2. The president earns $400,000.
3. The president is _____.
4. There are 50 states.
5. The largest city is New York City.
6. The population is about 321 million.

1790

1. New York City
2. $25,000
3. George Washington
4. 13 states
5. New York City
6. 3.9 million

ACTIVE GRAMMAR | Past Continuous: Statements and Questions

I	was	
He	was not	planting corn.
She	wasn't	driving a wagon.
You	were	reading to the children.
We	were not	cooking dinner.
They	weren't	

The past continuous can describe an action that was in progress at a specific time in the past.

They **were cooking** dinner at 6 o'clock.
I **was reading** to the children when I heard a noise.

A Complete the paragraph. Use the past continuous and the verbs in parentheses.

The Pilgrims

The Pilgrims were a religious group and one of the first groups of settlers in North America. They _____were living_____ (live) in England for many years, but they could not practice their religion. In 1620, they decided to sail to North America. They _____ (hope) to practice their religion. Their ship was named the Mayflower. The ship _____ (carry) 102 people, food, and small animals during the trip. While they _____ (cross) the Atlantic Ocean, many people became sick. They _____ (not / eat) well. They _____ (plan) to land in Virginia, but they landed on Cape Cod in the winter. Several Native American tribes _____ (live) there. While the Pilgrims were trying to survive their first year in America, a Native American man named Tisquantum, or "Squanto," _____ (teach) them how to grow corn. By 1627, the settlers _____ (do) well.

Was	I he she it	going to England?
Were	you we they	moving? planting vegetables?

What When Where Why	was	I he she it	eating? moving?
	were	you we they	crossing?

B Complete the questions. Use the past continuous and the words in parentheses.

1. (live / the Pilgrims) _____Were the Pilgrims living_____ in England?   Yes, they were.
2. What (carry / the ship) _____?   People, food, animals.
3. (eat / the Pilgrims) _____ well?   No, they weren't.
4. Where (plan / they) _____ to land?   Virginia.
5. What (teach / Tisquantum) _____ them to grow?   Corn.

ACTIVE GRAMMAR | *Used to*

I You We They He She	**used to**	**write** letters. **use** candles for light. **grow** vegetables.

> *Used to* can be used to talk about a habit or a routine that you had in the past but that you don't have now.
> **I used to drink** coffee.
> Now, I drink tea.

A **Pronunciation:** *Used to* Listen and repeat. 🎧 8

1. In colonial times, people used to drive horses and wagons.
2. People used to cook over open fires.
3. People used to grow their own food.
4. They used to write letters.
5. They used to attend very small schools.

B **CIVICS** Work with a partner. Read about life today and talk about life in Colonial America. Use the words in the box and *used to*.

candlelight	one-room schoolhouses
leather boots	spoons and knives
~~long dresses~~	wooden cups

1. Today, girls wear jeans, dresses, or skirts. *In colonial times, girls used to wear long dresses.*
2. Today, people drink from glasses.
3. Today, most children study in large public schools.
4. Today, most children wear sneakers.
5. Today, people read by electric lights.
6. Today, people eat with forks, knives, and spoons.

C Complete the sentences about life in your native country. Then, read your sentences to a partner.

1. When I lived in _____, I used to _____.
2. My family and I used to _____ every summer.
3. My friends and I used to _____ on Saturday nights.
4. I used to eat typical foods like _____.
5. I never used to _____.

ACTIVE GRAMMAR Simple Past: Questions

Did	I you we they he she	**live**	in the city?
Was	I she he it	interesting? at school? cold? in the city?
Were	you we they	

Where When How What time	**did**	I you we they he she	**go** to school?
How long		it	**take**?

More information in Appendix A.

A **ACADEMIC** Complete the questions. Then, listen to Eric talk about his childhood. Take notes in your notebook and answer the questions. 🎧9

1. _____Was_____ (be) he born in the United States?

2. _____ (do) he _____ (have) a big family?

3. _____ (be) he the oldest?

4. _____ (be) his relatives nearby?

5. _____ (do) he _____ (live) in the city or in the country?

6. _____ (do) he _____ (walk) to school?

7. _____ (be) he free in the summer?

8. _____ (be) his grandmother a good cook?

B Complete the questions. Use *did*, *was*, or *were*. Then, ask and answer the questions with a partner.

1. Where _____did_____ you live?

2. _____ there many children in your neighborhood?

3. _____ your home near the city or in the countryside?

4. What sports _____ you play?

5. _____ you like school?

6. What _____ your favorite activities?

7. When _____ you begin to study English?

ACTIVE GRAMMAR — *Who* Questions in the Past

Simple Past	Subject	Who			called?	His mother called.
	Object	Who	did	he	call?	He called his brother.
Past Continuous	Subject	Who	was		waiting?	His brother was waiting.
	Object	Who	was	he	waiting for?	He was waiting for a friend.

A Write the answers to these questions in your notebook. Use complete sentences.

1. Who did you come to this country with?
2. Who did you call after you arrived here?
3. Who did you ask for help finding a place to live?
4. Who did you talk to when you had a problem?
5. Who were you working with in class last week?
6. Who were you talking to before class today?

B Write two more *who* questions that ask about objects. Write one in the simple past and one in the past continuous. Ask a partner your questions.

1. _____

2. _____

C **AT WORK** Work in groups. Ask and answer the questions. Write the name of the student or students.

1. Who had a long trip to come to this country?   _____
2. Who was working before moving to the US?   _____
3. Who found a job right away?   _____
4. Who wanted to study English before getting a job?   _____
5. Who was studying English before coming to the US?   _____
6. Who knew how to drive before coming to this country?   _____

D Write two more *who* questions that ask about subjects. Write one in the simple past and one in the past continuous. Ask your classmates your questions.

1. _____

2. _____

THE BIG PICTURE / Benjamin Franklin

A **CIVICS** Listen and complete the outline of Benjamin Franklin's life. 🎧 10

A statue of Benjamin Franklin on the University of Pennsylvania campus in Philadelphia.

1. **Early life**

    a. Born in _____*Boston*_____ on ___*Jan. 17, 1706*___

    b. Attended school for _____ years

    c. Trained to become a _____

    d. Moved to _____

    e. Opened a _____

> When you listen to a lecture, take notes, but don't write down everything you hear. Only write the important information. You can write key words and phrases instead of complete sentences.

2. **Improvements to Philadelphia**

    a. Started the first _____

    b. Helped to organize the first _____

    c. Served as _____ and set up _____

    d. Encouraged city officials to pave the _____

3. **Three inventions**

    | bifocals lightning rod odometer |

a. _____ **b.** _____ **c.** _____

4. **Contributions as a leader**

   a. Signed the Declaration of _____

   | independence (noun) |
   | independent (adjective) |

   i. It stated that the 13 colonies were a _____ and _____ nation.

   b. Served as minister to _____

   c. Signed the Constitution

   i. It established a new _____.

5. **Death**

   a. Died on _____

B **CIVICS** Look at your outline. Work with a partner. Ask and answer the questions.

1. Where was Benjamin Franklin born?
2. How long did he attend school?
3. What trade did he learn?
4. What city did he move to?
5. What services did Franklin help to start?
6. What did he encourage city officials to do?
7. What did he invent to measure distance?
8. What important documents did he sign?
9. What did the Declaration of Independence say?
10. When did he die?

C Read the answers. Then, complete the questions.

1. **A:** When _was Benjamin Franklin born_ ?

   B: He was born in 1706.

2. **A:** _____ from high school?

   B: No, he didn't graduate from high school.

3. **A:** How many languages _____?

   B: He spoke five languages.

4. **A:** What _____ to help people see?

   B: He invented bifocals.

5. **A:** What _____ with?

   B: He experimented with electricity.

Plimoth Plantation

On November 11th, 1620, a small ship of people arrived in Plymouth, Massachusetts and started the second colony in America. These settlers were looking for a better life and religious freedom. Today, Plymouth is a popular **destination** for people who want to know more about the history of the United States.

One of the most popular **attractions** in Plymouth is Plimoth Plantation. Plimoth Plantation was the dream of Henry Hornblower II. When he was a boy, Hornblower used to read stories about the Pilgrims who lived in Plymouth. When he was older, he worked with **archaeologists** in the historic town. The archaeologists found many **artifacts** from the original colony. At the same time, historians were learning about the lives of the early colonists by reading their journals. In 1945, Henry Hornblower's father gave $20,000 to the Pilgrim Society to begin the **reconstruction** of Plimoth Plantation.

The Society made **reproductions** of the clothes, tools, furniture, and houses of the 1620s. The museum opened in 1947 with just two reproductions of colonial homes.

Today, Plimoth Plantation looks like the original settlement of 1627. It is a living museum of reconstructed homes, shops, and gardens. Visitors can walk through the colonial town where each house looks exactly like a house of the 1620s. The museum staff are the "colonists." They wear the same kinds of clothes as the Plymouth colonists used to wear. The women cook on open fireplaces and make colonial recipes. The men grow the same vegetables and raise the same animals as people used to do in colonial times. Everyone uses the same kinds of tools as the colonists used. The "colonists" talk to visitors using the same English language and accent of the original colonists. A trip to Plimoth Plantation is a trip back in history. 🎧 11

Kelley Araujo acts as colonist Julianna Kempton while talking with visitors in her garden at Plimoth Plantation.

A Name one historic place in your country. Why is it famous?

READING NOTE

Guessing the Meanings of New Words
It is often possible to guess the meaning of a new word by using the other words and phrases around it. When you see a new word, read the sentence again. Is the new word a verb, an adjective, or a noun? If you can't guess its meaning, read the sentences before and after the word.

B **ACADEMIC** Scan the text to find the words (1–6). Then, match the words with their meanings (a–f).

_____f_____ **1.** destination   **a.** copies of original items

_____ **2.** attractions   **b.** items or pieces of items from the past

_____ **3.** artifacts   **c.** people who study old objects to learn about the past

_____ **4.** archaeologists   **d.** interesting or enjoyable things that people want to see or do

_____ **5.** reconstruction   **e.** something that is put together again or rebuilt

_____ **6.** reproductions   **f.** a place that someone or something is going to

C Read the text.

D **ACADEMIC** Answer the questions.

1. Why did the colonists leave England?

2. Was Plymouth, Massachusetts the first colony?

3. How did Henry Hornblower find out about the Pilgrims at Plymouth?

4. What did archaeologists find at the site?

5. How did historians learn about the colonists' lives?

6. Why is Plimoth Plantation "a living museum"?

7. What do the "colonists" wear?

8. What kind of vegetables do they grow on Plimoth Plantation?

E Complete the sentences using words from the box.

| archaeologist | artifacts | ~~attraction~~ | destinations | reconstruction | reproductions |

1. Another popular _____attraction_____ in Plymouth is the Pilgrim Hall Museum.

2. Today, on Plimoth Plantation, museum staff use _____ of tools from colonial times so visitors can see what the original tools looked like.

3. There are many _____ in Massachusetts, such as Boston and Salem, where people can learn about US history.

4. Working as an _____ is a good job for someone who likes to learn about the past.

5. Henry Hornblower wanted to build a _____ of Plimoth Plantation.

6. Some workers found _____ from a Native American tribe.

A Read.

Laura Guigliano

October 18

The History of Pompeii

I am from Naples, Italy. It's in the southern part of Italy. A popular historic city in my area is Pompeii. Pompeii is near the Bay of Naples, and it is at the foot of an active volcano, Mount Vesuvius.

In 79 AD, the volcano erupted. Hot lava came out of the volcano and went down into the sea and the towns. The lava completely covered Pompeii, and many people died.

In 1738, workers discovered artifacts from Pompeii. They immediately told the city administration what they had found. Archaeologists and other experts went to the city. After many years of work, these experts uncovered the ancient city of Pompeii.

Pompeii used to be a popular vacation city for wealthy people from Rome. There used to be homes with beautiful gardens, shops, and places for entertainment. People used to spend time at the large outdoor theater. Today, visitors can walk around many parts of the city and look at the old homes. Many of the streets are still in good condition. Visitors can see many of the artifacts at the Naples National Archaeological Museum.

Some of the artifacts discovered at Pompeii include paintings, sculptures, jewelry, medical tools, and preserved food items.

Brainstorming

Before writing, it is helpful to think about your topic. Many writers **brainstorm**. This means that they write down all their ideas. Then, they use the ideas that they like best.

B Read Laura's brainstorming notes. Circle the ideas she used in her text.

Historic Place	Location	What is it?
the Colosseum	Rome	old stadium; place for entertainment for Romans; original seating; lots of tourists; cats
Pompeii	near Naples and Mt. Vesuvius	old city buried by lava from volcano; old homes, streets, gardens; outdoor theater and artifacts

C **ACADEMIC** Brainstorm historic places in your native country. Include the names and locations of a few places, what they are, what visitors do there, and other important information. If you need more information, search for it online. Take notes.

D Choose a historic place from your notes to write about. Use your own words to write your text.

E Read your partner's text. What historic place did your partner write about? Where is it? What can tourists see and do there?

F Find and correct the verb mistakes.

1. Benjamin Franklin ~~help~~ *helped* to improve the city of Philadelphia.

2. Did Philadelphia a major city?

3. When Washington become the capital?

4. Pompeii use to be a popular vacation city for wealthy people from Rome.

5. People living happy lives in Pompeii before the volcano erupted.

6. Who were the president of the United States in 1790?

7. The original settlers didn't knew how to grow their own food.

8. People used to traveled by ship from country to country.

A **AT WORK** Read the tips for giving a presentation. Then, write each sentence under the correct picture.

Giving a presentation takes a lot of practice. Here are some tips for giving a good presentation.

- Use an outline or note cards. Don't read your presentation.
- Make eye contact with the audience.
- Smile and greet your audience.
- Practice your presentation.
- Thank your audience.
- Use visuals.

WORD PARTNERSHIPS	
give	
listen to	a presentation
practice	

1.

Practice your presentation.

4.

_____

2.

_____

5.

_____

3.

_____

6.

_____

B **AT WORK** Prepare a presentation for your class. Use the information from the text you wrote about a historic place. Remember the tips for giving a presentation listed above.

CHANGING LIFESTYLES

AT WORK Distinguish appropriate responses to workplace scenarios; describe future career plans; set a goal and identify steps to achieve it

ACADEMIC Identify key phrases in a text; infer the meaning of new vocabulary from context; organize a sequence of events; identify and use transition words to organize writing

CIVICS Read and interpret ads for housing; select appropriate housing based on information provided

Triplets Alama, Olympia, and Donata attend a triplets meetup in Neu-Anspach, Germany.

A Work in groups. Talk about what is happening in each picture.

Kelly _____

Sabrina _____

Hugo _____

James and Carla _____

Laura _____

Ahmed _____

Dan _____ 1 _____

Amy and Tom _____

Sofia _____

B Listen and write the number for each person's plan(s) under the correct picture. 🎧12

C With a partner, ask and answer the questions about the future plans from the previous exercise.

> Who is going to save money for a house?

> James and Carla are.

1. Who is going to save money for a house?
2. Who will email their family every day?
3. Who is going to register for courses?
4. Who is going to vote in the next election?
5. Who will get two months of maternity leave?

ACTIVE GRAMMAR | Future with *be going to:* Statements

I	am 'm am not 'm not		move. change jobs. get married. have a baby.
You We They	are 're are not 're not / aren't	going to	
He She	is 's		
It	is not 's not / isn't		rain.

We can use *be going to* to talk about future plans.

More information in Appendix A.

A Listen. Complete the sentences. Some of the sentences are negative. 🎧13

1. Julie and Ellie _____ *are not / aren't going to go* _____ away to college.

2. Julie and Ellie _____ to community college.

3. Julie _____ education like her mother did.

4. She _____ engineering and architecture.

5. Ellie _____ a counselor on Monday.

6. Julie _____ full time.

7. She _____ at a department store, and

   she _____ classes at night.

8. They _____ the same schedule.

9. Ellie _____ classes at night because

   she _____ at her father's restaurant.

B Look at the pictures on the previous page. With a partner, discuss how each person's life is going to change.

> Kelly is going to look for an apartment.

> Kelly is going to get a job.

Am	I			
Are	you we they	**going to**	move? change jobs? go to college? get married?	
Is	he she			
	it		rain?	

What **are** you **going to** do?
How **are** we **going to** get there?
Where **are** they **going to** move?
Who **is** she **going to** visit?
Who **is going to** help?
When **is** it **going to** rain?

More information in Appendix A.

A **LET'S TALK.** Ask your classmates *Yes / No* questions about their future plans using *be going to*. When someone answers "Yes, I am," write their name on the line. If someone answers "No, I'm not," ask another classmate.

1. work this weekend? _____
2. move this year? _____
3. visit your native country soon? _____
4. buy a house this year? _____
5. work out today? _____
6. celebrate a special occasion this month? _____
7. look for a new job soon? _____
8. eat out this weekend? _____

B With a partner, ask and answer questions about your weekend plans. Use words from the box or your own ideas.

clean	go to a party	see a movie
go dancing	go to (a place)	visit a friend
go shopping	play (a sport)	work

My family and I are going to go to a wedding this weekend.

Who's going to get married?
Where's the wedding going to be?
What are you going to wear?

ACTIVE GRAMMAR | Present Continuous with Future Meaning

If a specific time in the future is stated or clear, the present continuous can express future time.

I**'m working** tomorrow.
He **is leaving** at 4:00.

Sofia is at the community college registration office.

A It's 9:00 a.m. on Monday, and Sofia is getting information about courses. Write about Sofia's plans using the present continuous and the words below.

1. Sofia / go / to an orientation / at 10 a.m.
   Sofia is going to an orientation at 10 a.m.

2. Sofia / take / a tour of the campus / after the orientation
   _____

3. She / meet / a friend / for lunch / in the cafeteria at 12:30
   _____

4. Sofia / talk / to a counselor / this afternoon
   _____

5. Sofia / sign up / for courses / after she speaks with the counselor
   _____

6. Sofia / not buy / textbooks / until she receives her class schedule
   _____

7. Sofia / not work / tomorrow
   _____

8. Sofia and her husband / go shopping / for school supplies / tomorrow afternoon
   _____

B Listen and circle the meaning. 🎧14

1. (Now)   Future   4. Now   Future   7. Now   Future
2. Now   Future   5. Now   Future   8. Now   Future
3. Now   Future   6. Now   Future   9. Now   Future

Will can be used to make an offer or a decision at the time of action.
It is common to use the contraction *'ll*.
   I**'ll** help you.
   They**'ll** fix it.

A **Pronunciation: *'ll*** Listen and repeat. 🎧15

1. I'll do it.
2. I'll get it.
3. I'll call you.

4. I'll help him.
5. I'll be there.
6. They'll paint it.

7. She'll do it.
8. He'll answer it.
9. We'll help you.

B Work with a partner. Take turns reading the statements and offering to help by using the expressions in the box.

change it	give you directions	read it
explain it	help you look	show you how
~~give you a ride~~	introduce you	translate it

My car broke down, and I don't have a ride to school.

I'll give you a ride.

1. My car broke down, and I don't have a ride to school.

2. I can't find my keys.

3. I don't know how to use my new smart TV.

4. I just moved in, and I don't know anyone around here.

5. I don't know how to get to the mall.

6. I wrote this report, but I need someone to read it over for me.

7. I received a letter in English, but I don't understand it.

8. My car has a flat tire.

9. My income taxes are due next week, but I don't know how to fill out the form.

> *Will* can also be used to make a promise.
> The negative form of *will* is *will not* or *won't*.
>> I **will** call you as soon as I arrive.
>> We **will not** text in class again.
>> He **won't** do that anymore.

> Both *will / won't* and *be (not) going to* can be used to make predictions.
>> New cars **are going to** use less gas.
>> There **will** be more self-driving cars on the road.

C **AT WORK** **LET'S TALK.** With a partner, answer the question about each photo. Use your imagination. Try to make one affirmative and one negative sentence.

1. What promises is he making to his father? *I won't text and drive again.*

3. What promises is he making to his manager?

2. What promises are the girls making?

4. What promises are the boys going to make?

D Make predictions about the future of cars.

1. There will be more cars that use _____.

2. There will be less _____.

3. There will be more _____.

4. More people _____.

5. The number of cars on the road _____.

After I **study** hard for two years, I**'ll** graduate.
(time clause)   (main clause)
When I **have** time, I**'m going to** finish my degree.
(time clause)   (main clause)
I**'ll** graduate after I **study** hard for two years.
(main clause)   (time clause)
I**'m going to** finish my degree when I **have** time.
(main clause)   (time clause)

1. A time clause can begin with words such as *after, before, when,* and *if.*
2. Use a comma when the time clause is at the beginning of a sentence. Do not use a comma when the time clause is at the end of a sentence.

More information in Appendix A.

A | **AT WORK** | Find the best matches to complete the sentences about Sonia's plans.

_____b_____ **1.** If Sonia works hard at her job,

_____ **2.** When Sonia takes a vacation,

_____ **3.** After Sonia saves some money,

_____ **4.** If Sonia meets the right person,

_____ **5.** After Sonia interviews for several jobs,

a. she'll buy a new car.

b. she'll get a promotion.

c. she'll accept the best offer.

d. she'll travel around Europe.

e. she'll get married.

B | **AT WORK** | Complete the sentences about Sonia's future. Use your imagination.

1. Before Sonia gets married, _____.

2. _____ when she has children.

3. If she decides to become a stay-at-home mom, _____.

4. _____ after her children are grown.

5. If Sonia decides to change careers, _____.

6. When Sonia has enough money, _____.

7. _____ when she retires.

8. _____.

9. _____.

C **LET'S TALK.** With a partner, ask and answer the questions. Make future time clauses using *before, after, if,* or *when.*

> When are you going to get married?

> I'm going to get married after I graduate from college.

1. When are you going to travel out of the country?

2. When are you going to buy a new car?

3. When are you going to move into a bigger place?

4. When are you going to pay your utility bills?

5. When are you going to take a day off from work?

6. When are you going to become a US citizen?

7. When are you going to leave this classroom?

D **ACADEMIC** **LET'S TALK.** With a partner, number the events in George's life in order from 1 to 8. Then, make sentences about his life using *before, after,* and *when.*

> George is going to graduate from college before he finds a job.

> After George meets someone special, he's going to get married.

find a job

buy a house

get married

graduate from college

have a daughter

have a son

meet someone special

save a lot of money

A Laura is expecting her first child. How do you think her life is going to change after the baby comes? Discuss Laura's plans for the items below. Use your imagination.

- work
- apartment / house
- free time

WORD PARTNERSHIPS	
maternity paternity family	leave
stay-at-home	dad mom

B Listen. Circle the changes that Laura and her husband, Brady, are going to make. 🎧 16

buy a house	get a cat	stay home
change work schedules	give away their cats	take a class
change jobs	go out three nights a week	take some time off
find a bigger apartment	move	

C Listen again and circle *True* or *False*. 🎧 16

1.	They're still looking for a house.	True	(False)
2.	They like their building.	True	False
3.	They're going to move soon.	True	False
4.	Some of the houses that they looked at needed work.	True	False
5.	Their building is far from Laura's work.	True	False
6.	She's going to take off two weeks from work.	True	False
7.	Laura and Brady are going to go out less often.	True	False

D Find the best matches to complete the sentences.

_____d___ **1.** If they like the bigger apartment,

_____ **2.** When the baby arrives,

_____ **3.** They're going to do a lot of shopping

_____ **4.** When Laura's maternity leave begins,

_____ **5.** They're going to move

_____ **6.** Laura will call Melissa

a. before the baby comes.

b. Laura's mother is going to help.

c. if she needs help.

d. they'll move as soon as possible.

e. after they find a bigger apartment.

f. she'll stay at home.

E Complete the sentences. Use the simple past, simple present, present continuous, future, or *going to*.

1. Melissa (give) _____ *gave* _____ Laura a baby shower.

2. Laura's company (give) _____ her two months of maternity leave.

3. They (not / want) _____ to move out of their building.

4. Laura and Brady (take) _____ a parenting class now.

5. They (not / get) _____ rid of their cats.

6. Her mother (help) _____ after the baby is born.

7. Brady (not / take) _____ a lot of time off from work.

8. Laura's mother (take) _____
care of the baby when Laura (go)_____ back to work.

Empty Nesters

Parents whose children have recently left home are called *empty nesters*. Their little birds, or children, have flown away to start independent lives. This is a big **adjustment**, or change, for the parents. They often feel lonely or depressed after their children become more independent. This condition is called *empty nest* **syndrome**.

Sights and sounds can **trigger** the condition. A parent may suddenly start to feel sad. One mother said, "I drove past my son's soccer field the other day and suddenly started crying." One father reported that he had to pull over to the side of the road after he heard his daughter's favorite song on the radio. "I never thought I would miss her so much," he said.

Children do not have to move out of the house for parents to experience empty nest syndrome. When children enter high school, they may start going out on weekends and playing sports. Some parents only see their children at breakfast or on their way out of the house. They find it difficult to **cope with**, or handle, their children's independence, and they miss how close they used to be.

When parents do not recover from their sad feelings after a few months, they may want to **seek** professional help. In addition, they may look for assistance online, such as support groups, to help them through this difficult transition.

Fortunately, empty nest syndrome passes with time. Most parents actually find that an empty nest allows them more time to do the things they love, like travel. In fact, the **majority** of empty nesters say that they travel more frequently. Also, they don't need to plan trips around school vacation weeks, when prices are higher. In addition to travel, empty nesters can enjoy new hobbies or volunteer work. Cellphones and social media help parents to keep in touch with their children. So empty nesters can stay connected while having exciting new experiences and taking time for themselves. 🎧17

An incoming student and her mother check their program schedules at George Washington University's freshman orientation.

A Discuss the questions with a partner.

1. Do you have any children? If so, how old are they?

2. At what age do you think children are ready to live on their own?

3. How do you think parents feel when their children move away from home?

> **READING NOTE**
>
> **Finding Vocabulary Definitions**
> Sometimes, you can find the definitions of new words in the text. After the new word, look for a comma and then a word or short phrase that gives the definition. The sentences before or after the new word can also give clues about its meaning.

B **ACADEMIC** Find the words in the reading. Then, write the definitions.

1. adjustment _____*change*_____   4. cope with _____
2. syndrome _____   5. seek _____
3. trigger _____   6. majority _____

C Read the text.

D Circle *True* or *False*.

1.	Empty nest syndrome is a problem for college students.	True	(False)
2.	Only sights can trigger a parent to feel sad.	True	False
3.	Both mothers and fathers can experience this syndrome.	True	False
4.	One parent became upset after she heard her son's voice.	True	False
5.	Parents with high-school-age children can also be empty nesters.	True	False
6.	High school children always spend a lot of time with their parents.	True	False
7.	There is professional help for empty nesters.	True	False
8.	Most empty nesters travel more often than they did before.	True	False

E **ACADEMIC** In your own words, write a definition of empty nest syndrome in your notebook.

A Read.

Carlos Garcia

October 15

My Goal

I am an ESL student at Union County College. I came from Cuba three years ago. When I first came here, I did not speak any English, but now I can carry on a conversation in English and understand most people. I work at a warehouse, but only a few people speak English there. My goal is to improve my speaking. I am going to make some changes so that I will speak English much more fluently.

<u>First of all</u>, I will look for a job where I can use English more often. After I start my new job, I am going to ask my coworkers to correct my English. I think it is important to know when I make a mistake so that I can learn from it. Next, I think I will register for a pronunciation class because many people do not understand me the first time I say something. Then, I am going to try to find a study partner who speaks a different language. Finally, I am going to start shopping at stores where I will have to speak English. If I do these things, I think my English will improve, and I will achieve my goal.

WRITING NOTE

Transition Words

Use transition words to explain the steps of a plan or to describe the order of your ideas. Use a comma after a transition word when it begins a sentence. Here are some transition words and phrases:

First,   First of all,   Second,   Third,   Fourth,   Next,
Then,   After,   After that,   Finally,   Last,

B **ACADEMIC** Underline the transition words in the text above.

C **ACADEMIC** Number the sentences in the correct order.

_____ When I arrive at work, I'll take the stairs.

___1___ My goal is to get in better shape.

_____ I'll eat a light dinner, and I won't eat after 7:00 p.m.

_____ I'm going to eat a healthy lunch and drink water or tea.

_____ During my breaks, I'll walk around the halls of the office.

_____ After work, I'm going to go to the gym.

D **ACADEMIC** In your notebook, write the sentences from Exercise C in order in a paragraph. Use transition words.

E **AT WORK** Write about one of your professional or personal goals. Use transition words. Answer these questions in your text.

1. What is one of your goals?

2. What steps are you going to take to achieve this goal?

3. How long do you think it will take to achieve this goal?

F Read a partner's text. What is his or her goal? Underline the transition words.

G Find and correct the verb mistakes.

1. In ten years, there ~~are~~ *will be* many more hybrid cars.

2. Before I quit this job, I going to find a new one.

3. He's going to stay home with his children if he will lose his job.

4. Is she going to go to college when she leave the military?

5. I took the citizenship test tomorrow at 4:00.

6. I pick it up for you.

7. Where they are going to live?

8. They need a bigger apartment if they have another child.

A **CIVICS** Match each person or family with the home you think is best for them. Compare your answers with a partner. Then, go online and search for a house or apartment that you think might be good for you. Discuss your choice with your classmates.

1. We have a one-bedroom apartment. We are expecting another child, so we need a bigger place. We want a house with a yard and a garage.
Home _____

2. Our children are grown, and our house is too big. We don't need four bedrooms or a yard. We want something smaller.
Home _____

3. I have a full-time job, and I'm ready to buy a home. I'd like a one-bedroom apartment with parking.
Home _____

a. $339,000, 3 beds, 2½ baths, gas heat, fireplace, garage, near parks, schools, and transportation; built 1960s

b. $249,000, 2 beds, 2 baths, A/C, gas heat, parking, tennis courts, near schools, shopping, and transportation

c. $199,999, 1 bed, 1 bath, A/C, gas heat, gym, pool, 24-hr doorman, near shops, transportation; built 90s

d. $329,000, 2 beds, 2 baths, finished basement, oil heat, garage, near shopping; built 70s

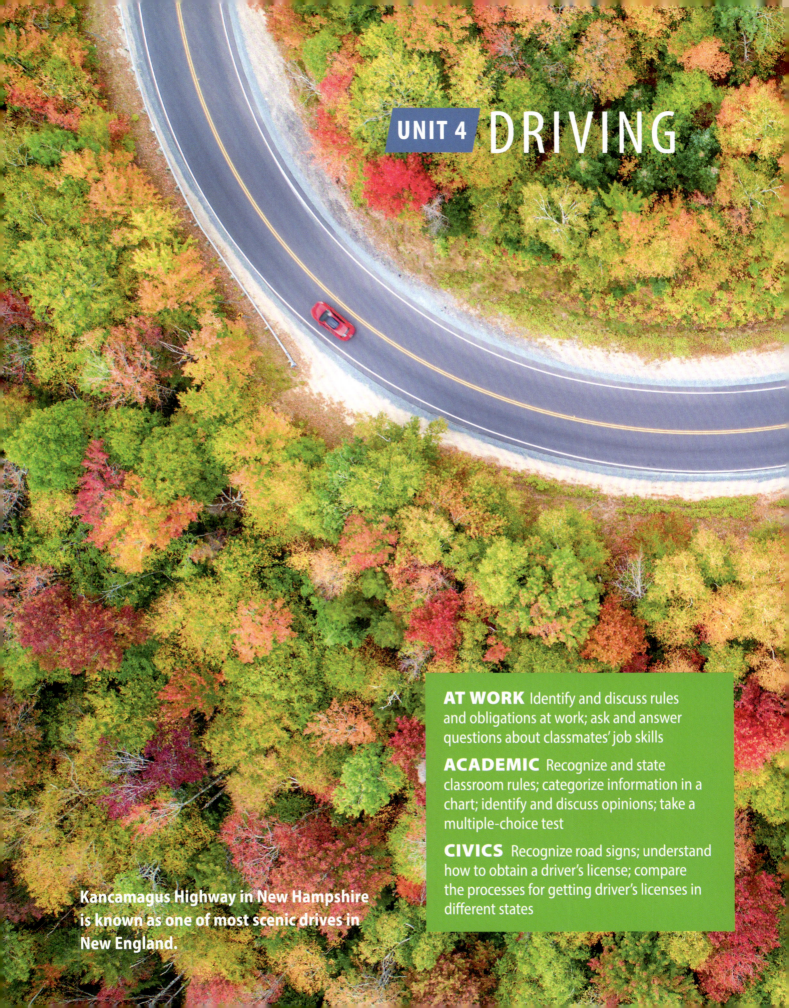

UNIT 4 DRIVING

AT WORK Identify and discuss rules and obligations at work; ask and answer questions about classmates' job skills

ACADEMIC Recognize and state classroom rules; categorize information in a chart; identify and discuss opinions; take a multiple-choice test

CIVICS Recognize road signs; understand how to obtain a driver's license; compare the processes for getting driver's licenses in different states

Kancamagus Highway in New Hampshire is known as one of most scenic drives in New England.

A **CIVICS** Match each traffic rule with the correct sign.

a. You must not ride bikes here.

b. Trucks must not use this road.

c. You must not turn left.

d. You must stop for pedestrians.

e. You must not park here or you will be towed.

f. You must stay to the right.

g. You must look out for deer.

h. You must slow down. This is a school zone.

i. You must not park here.

j. You must slow down. The road is slippery when wet.

k. You must slow down and be prepared to stop. There is construction ahead.

l. You must turn right. This is a one-way street.

1. _____ f _____

2. _____

3. _____

4. _____

5. _____

6. _____

7. _____

8. _____

9. _____

10. _____

11. _____

12. _____

ACTIVE GRAMMAR — Modals: *Must / Must not*

| I
You
We
They
He
She | **must** | **stop** at a red light.
drive under the speed limit. |
| | **must not** | **drive** without a license. |

We can use *must* to describe rules, obligation, or necessity.

    Drivers **must stop** at stop signs.

We can use *must not* to describe an action that is not permitted.

    You **must not drive** through red lights.

More information in Appendix A.

A Use each sentence to state a traffic law. Use *must* or *must not*.

> You must stop at a stop sign.

> You must not pass cars on the right.

1. Stop at a stop sign.

2. Don't pass cars on the right.

3. Pay traffic fines.

4. Don't drink alcohol and drive.

5. Register your car.

6. Don't drive over the speed limit.

7. Wear your seat belt.

8. Stop for a school bus with flashing lights.

9. Don't drive without a license.

B **ACADEMIC** Read each school rule. Check *Yes* or *No* for your school.

School Rules	Yes	No
1. We must arrive on time.		
2. We must call or email our teacher if we are absent.		
3. We must wear uniforms.		
4. We must speak English all the time.		
5. We must not copy from other students.		
6. We must not eat in class.		

C **ACADEMIC** In your notebook, write three more rules for your school or class.

I You We They	have to	wear a seat belt.
	do not have to / don't have to	buy a new car.
He She	has to	drive with a license.
	does not have to / doesn't have to	wash the car.

Have to can describe necessity or obligation.

I **have to get** car insurance.

Doesn't have to / don't have to can describe something that is not necessary.

She **doesn't have to go** to school on Sundays.

More information in Appendix A.

A Look at the pictures and complete the sentences. Use *have to* or *has to* and an appropriate verb.

1. She _____ has to move _____ her car.
2. She _____ the ticket.

3. He _____ the tires.
4. He _____ new tires.

5. They _____ their sports car.
6. They _____ a car seat for their baby.

B Restate each sentence. Use *doesn't have to* or *don't have to.*

1. It's not necessary for a person to speak English to get a driver's license.

2. It's not necessary for you to have a radio in your car.

> A person doesn't have to speak English to get a driver's license.

3. It's not necessary for new drivers to have jobs.

4. It's not necessary for a new learner to go to a private driving school.

5. It's not necessary for drivers to have cellphones.

6. It's not necessary for you to wash your car every day.

C **AT WORK** Complete the sentences. Use *must not* (not permitted) or *doesn't have to / don't have to* (not necessary).

1. Employees _____*don't have to*_____ buy food in the company cafeteria because there are many restaurants nearby.

2. I _____*must not*_____ arrive late to work.

3. I _____ wear a suit or a dress to my job.

4. An employee _____ respond to emails after 6 p.m.

5. Workers _____ smoke in the workplace.

6. Employees at my office _____ work on the weekends.

7. We _____ use our cellphones for personal calls at work.

8. An employee _____ take home supplies from work.

9. Employees _____ take vacation time without telling the manager.

D **ACADEMIC** Listen to Rebecca talking about her to-do list. Check the tasks that she has completed. 🎧 18

Tasks	Completed
1. buy stamps	
2. mail a package	
3. do laundry	
4. go to the supermarket	
5. make a deposit at the bank	
6. confirm an appointment	
7. put gas in her car	

E Ask and answer questions about Rebecca's to-do list. Use the information in Exercise D.

Do	I you we they	have to	**clean** the floor? **buy** stamps? **see** the dentist?
Does	he she		

Does Rebecca have to buy stamps?

No, she doesn't. She bought some yesterday.

I You We They He She	can cannot can't	drive. park in this area.

More information in Appendix A.

We can use *can* to describe ability. We can use *cannot / can't* to describe inability.

I **can drive** a car, but I **can't drive** a truck.

We can also use *can* to describe a permitted action. We can use *cannot / can't* to describe an action that is not permitted.

I **can drive** at night by myself.

You **can't drive** through red lights.

A **Pronunciation: *Can* and *Can't*** Listen. Complete the sentences with *can* or *can't*. 🎧 19

1. Marcus _____can't_____ drive very well.
2. He _____ back up.
3. He _____ parallel park.
4. He _____ only drive with a licensed driver in the car.
5. He _____ drive on the highway.
6. He _____ drive late at night.
7. He _____ drive with the radio on.

B **AT WORK** **LET'S TALK.** Ask your classmates *Yes / No* questions about their job skills. If someone answers, "Yes, I can," write their name in the chart. If someone answers, "No, I can't," ask another person.

Question	Name
1. drive a truck	
2. use a cash register	
3. change a tire	
4. cook well	
5. type fast	
6. speak Spanish	

Can you drive a truck?

Yes, I can.

Around 3.5 million truck drivers are employed in the United States.

ACTIVE GRAMMAR | Modals: *Could / Couldn't*

I You We	**could**	**speak** English. **walk** to school.
They He She	**could not** **couldn't**	**drive** a car.

We can use *could* to describe past ability. We can use *could not / couldn't* to describe past inability.

I **could drive** when I came to this country.

I **couldn't speak** English when I arrived in the US.

A Complete the sentences about yourself. Use *could* or *couldn't* and the verbs below.

1. When I came to this country, I (speak) _____ English.

2. When I came to this country, I (understand) _____ English.

3. When I came to this country, I (read) _____ a book without a dictionary.

4. When I came to this country, I (cook) _____ American food.

5. When I came here, I (drive) _____ a car.

6. When I came here, I (use) _____ a computer.

B Complete the sentences using *could* or *couldn't*.

1. When I moved here, I _____.

2. When I started this English program, _____.

3. When I started this class, _____.

C With a partner, ask and answer questions about your first day in English class.

Could	I you we they he she	**speak** English? **find** a job? **use** the computer?

ask questions in English
do the first homework assignment
find a place to park
find the classroom
get your books
~~speak English~~
speak your language with the teacher
understand the teacher

Could you speak English on the first day?

Yes, I could speak a little English.

I You We They He She	should	
		drive at night.
	should not	**buy** that car.
	shouldn't	

We can use *should* to express an opinion or give advice.

> I **should buy** a smaller car. Small cars get good gas mileage.

We can use *should not / shouldn't* to show that something is not a good idea.

> You **shouldn't put** your packages in the back seat.
> You **should put** them in your trunk.

A **ACADEMIC** **LET'S TALK.** Read each statement. Check your opinion. Then, discuss your reasons in a small group.

> I agree that drivers should drive more carefully near elementary schools. Young children can run into the street.

Opinion	Agree	Disagree
1. Drivers should drive more carefully near elementary schools.		
2. Teenagers are too young to drive cars.		
3. Small children should always ride in the back seat of a car.		
4. People over 80 years old should not drive.		
5. Drivers should not eat and drive at the same time.		
6. The state should increase the speed limit on the highway.		

B Read the scenarios and give advice using *should* or *shouldn't*. Discuss your answers with a partner.

1. A family with five children needs a new car. What kind of car should they buy?

2. Chen wants to learn how to drive. Who should teach him?

3. Politicians are considering changing the minimum driving age from 16 to 20. Should they change the law or leave it as it is?

Should people over 80 years old be able to drive?

| I You We They He She | **had better** **'d better** | **wear** a seat belt. **use** a car seat. |
| | **had better not** **'d better not** | **drive** without a license. **forget** to fill the gas tank. |

Had better / had better not can express warnings. *Had better / had better not* are stronger than *should / shouldn't.*

You**'d better check** your tire.
(Or you'll get a flat tire.)
I**'d better not miss** another class.
(Or I'll fail the course.)

A **Pronunciation: *'d better / 'd better not*** Listen and complete the sentences. Then, listen again and repeat. 🎧 20

1. _____ I'd better stay _____ home. I don't feel well.

2. _____ the baby in the car seat.

3. _____ the police and report the accident.

4. _____ the party inside. It's beginning to rain.

5. _____ tonight. He's very tired.

6. _____ a dog. Your landlord won't allow it.

7. _____ down. The roads are icy.

8. _____ that. I can't afford it.

B **LET'S TALK.** Give warnings using *'d better* or *'d better not.*

1.

He'd better slow down.

2.

3.

4.

5.

6.

THE BIG PICTURE Getting a Driver's License

A CIVICS Jennifer is preparing to get her driver's license. She is talking about the rules in her state. Listen and complete the chart. 21

CULTURE NOTE

Each state has different rules for getting a driver's license.

DMV = Department of Motor Vehicles

1 → Pass D.A.T.A. (Drug, Alcohol, Traffic Awareness) course

2 → Application with ___parent___'s permission
+
Proof of ______________ and address
- ______________ certificate
- Permanent resident card
- Citizenship papers

+
Social ______________ card

3 → Written test ______%
- ______________ questions and signs
- ______________ languages

+
Vision test
E
ONZ
KPMFS
UENWOASF

4 →

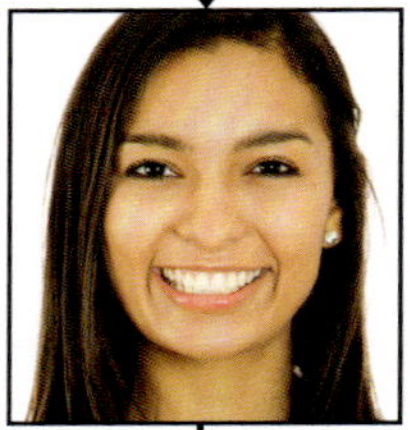

5 →
PERMIT
- $48.00
- Good for ______ years
- 50 hours' practice with adult ______ years+
- Includes 10 hours of practice at ______

6 → Licensed driver ______ years or older + ______________ ______________ card + Car registration + Permit

7 →
ROAD TEST

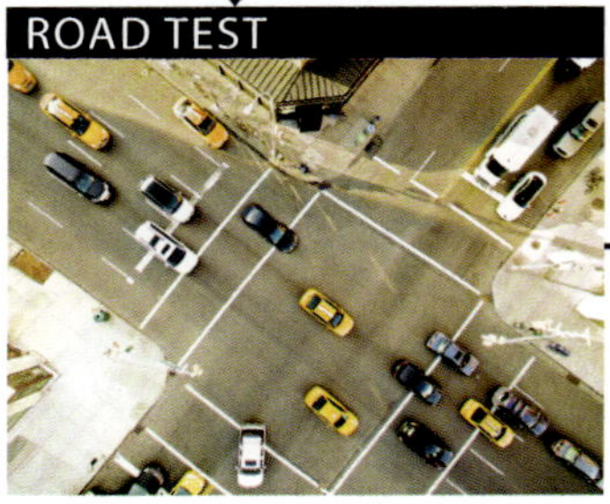

8 →

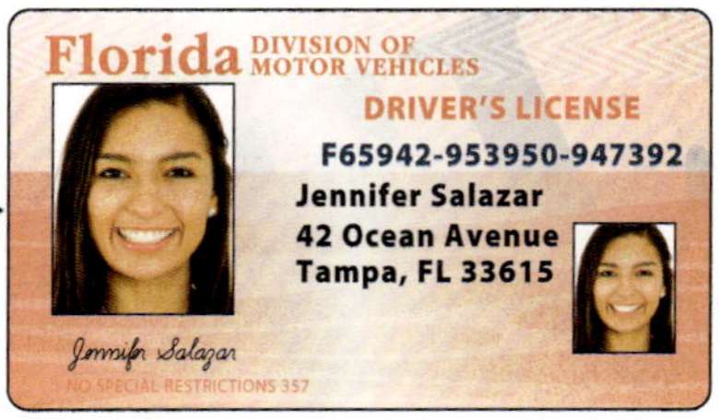

Florida DIVISION OF MOTOR VEHICLES
DRIVER'S LICENSE
F65942-953950-947392
Jennifer Salazar
42 Ocean Avenue
Tampa, FL 33615
Jennifer Salazar

B Circle *True* or *False*. Then, work with a partner. Take turns telling each other the correct information for each false statement.

1. Jennifer must take two tests before she gets her permit.   (True)   False

2. Jennifer has to show her birth certificate for proof of age.   True   False

3. Jennifer can take the written test in her native language.   True   False

4. Jennifer has to get 90 percent correct to pass the written test.   True   False

5. She can practice for two years with her permit.   True   False

6. Jennifer's sister can teach her how to drive.   True   False

7. Jennifer must drive with someone 21 or older.   True   False

8. Jennifer has to show an auto insurance card to take the road test.   True   False

9. Jennifer must go to the road test with a licensed driver.   True   False

C Ask and answer questions about the steps Jennifer must take to get a driver's license. Use the words below and modals like *have to, can,* and *should*.

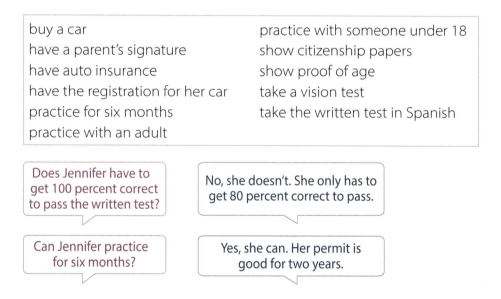

buy a car	practice with someone under 18
have a parent's signature	show citizenship papers
have auto insurance	show proof of age
have the registration for her car	take a vision test
practice for six months	take the written test in Spanish
practice with an adult	

Does Jennifer have to get 100 percent correct to pass the written test?

No, she doesn't. She only has to get 80 percent correct to pass.

Can Jennifer practice for six months?

Yes, she can. Her permit is good for two years.

D **CIVICS** Work in groups. Go online. Find information about the process for getting a driver's license in your state. Discuss the questions.

1. What do you need to do to get a learner's permit in your state? A driver's license?

2. How is the process the same or different from Jennifer's state?

A Discuss the questions.

1. Do you have a driver's license?

2. If you have a driver's license, did you take the written test in English?

3. What was the minimum passing score on the written test?

READING NOTE

Multiple-Choice Questions
When you take a multiple-choice test, read each choice carefully. Then, try to eliminate the choices you know are incorrect.

B **ACADEMIC** Read the sample driving test questions on the next page. Fill in the circle next to the correct answer.

●	⊗	✓	◖
Yes	**No**	**No**	**No**

C Check your answers below.

1. b   2. d   3. d   4. c   5. b   6. c   7. a   8. a   9. c   10. d

| **8 or more correct** | *Congratulations*! You pass. Get your learner's permit. |
| **Fewer than 8** | *Sorry*. You need more practice. Study the correct answers. Then, retake the test. |

A school crossing guard helps students cross a snowy street in Ontario, Canada.

The Written Driving Test

1. A driver approaching a flashing red traffic signal must. . .

   ○ **a.** drive carefully without stopping.
   ○ **b.** stop and then pass through.
   ○ **c.** stop and get out of the car.
   ○ **d.** slow down at the intersection.

2. You must stop your vehicle. . .

   ○ **a.** at an intersection with a stop sign.
   ○ **b.** where there is a red light.
   ○ **c.** when a traffic officer orders you to stop.
   ○ **d.** All of the above.

3. You must turn on your headlights. . .

   ○ **a.** when you turn on your wipers.
   ○ **b.** in the evening.
   ○ **c.** one half hour before sunset.
   ○ **d.** All of the above.

4. If you are driving behind a school bus and it shows a flashing red light, you must. . .

   ○ **a.** slow down.
   ○ **b.** slow down and pass on the left.
   ○ **c.** stop at least 25 feet away.
   ○ **d.** All of the above.

5. You are driving on a highway with a 65 mph speed limit. You may legally drive. . .

   ○ **a.** 70 mph or faster.
   ○ **b.** no faster than 65 mph.
   ○ **c.** between 65 and 70.
   ○ **d.** as fast as you'd like.

6. You have a green light, but the traffic is blocking the intersection. You must. . .

   ○ **a.** pass the traffic on the left.
   ○ **b.** honk your horn.
   ○ **c.** wait until the traffic clears. Then, go.
   ○ **d.** pass the traffic on the right.

7. You must obey the instructions of school crossing guards. . .

   ○ **a.** at all times.
   ○ **b.** when school is closed.
   ○ **c.** in the morning.
   ○ **d.** when it is raining.

8. If you pass your exit on a highway, you should. . .

   ○ **a.** go to the next exit.
   ○ **b.** stop immediately.
   ○ **c.** make a U-turn.
   ○ **d.** back up slowly to the exit that you want.

9. What does this sign mean?

   ○ **a.** Three-way intersection
   ○ **b.** Stop
   ○ **c.** Railroad crossing ahead
   ○ **d.** No turns

10. What does this sign mean?

    ○ **a.** One-way street ahead
    ○ **b.** Pass other cars on the right.
    ○ **c.** Left turn only
    ○ **d.** The road ahead is curvy. 22

A Read.

Marie Ceus

November 12

Safe Driving Near Elementary Schools

I think drivers should be more careful near elementary schools. One reason is that <u>there is a lot of traffic near elementary schools</u>, especially early in the morning and after school. At my son's school, it's very busy in the morning. Many parents drop off their children at school, and school buses come and go. In the afternoon, it's just as busy because the buses and the parents have to pick up the children, so there is a lot of traffic.

Another reason that drivers must be careful is that it's sometimes difficult to see small children near the cars. Some parents walk with their children to school, but other children can walk by themselves. A lot of drivers have large cars, and they can't see the children. Some children cross between the cars and behind the buses, so drivers must go slowly near schools. Sometimes, a child runs into the street without looking both ways.

The final reason is that some drivers don't pay attention or they are distracted by their cellphones. They had better put down their cellphones and pay closer attention to all the activity. In conclusion, drivers must be very careful when they drive near elementary schools.

In most states, the speed limit in school zones is between 15 and 25 mph.

SCHOOL BUS

STOP

130

B **ACADEMIC** Answer the questions about the text on the previous page.

1. The writer thinks that drivers should drive carefully near elementary schools. Underline the reasons.

2. Do you agree or disagree with the writer? Explain.

3. Did the writer use any modals (*must, can, could, should*) in this text? Find a sentence that uses modals and share it with the class.

WRITING NOTE

Writing Your Opinion

When you give your opinion, it is important to give your reasons. One way to introduce your reasons is to use the following expressions:

One reason is. . .   Another reason is. . .   The final reason is. . .

To end your writing, use one of the following expressions:

In conclusion,   In sum,   To sum up,

C **ACADEMIC** Choose one of your opinions from Exercise A on page 56. Write three reasons for your opinion here.

1. _____.

2. _____.

3. _____.

D **ACADEMIC** Write a paragraph about your opinion. Use your reasons from Exercise C and the expressions from the Writing Note.

E **ACADEMIC** Work with a partner. Read your partner's paragraph and number their reasons for their opinion. How many reasons does your partner give?

F Find and correct the mistakes.

1. She must ~~puts~~ *put* money in the parking meter.

2. Can you driving a stick shift?

3. Drivers has to follow the traffic rules.

4. I don't have to took the test in English.

5. He better not take another day off, or he'll lose his job.

6. We should buying a new car.

A   Listen and repeat. Then, write the letter of each car part next to the correct word. 🎧 23

___ 1. accelerator	___ 4. clutch	___ 7. signal	___ 9. gear shift	___ 12. windshield
___ 2. brake	_A_ 5. hood	___ 8. steering	___ 10. tires	___ 13. windshield
___ 3. bumper	___ 6. horn	wheel	___ 11. trunk	wipers

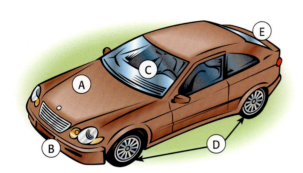

WORD PARTNERSHIPS	
check	the oil the tire pressure
replace	the filters the wiper blades

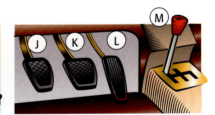

B   Complete the sentences. Use words from Exercise A.

1.   _____Windshield wipers_____ clean your windshield.

2.   A _____ can protect your car in minor accidents.

3.   When you want to go forward or faster, press the _____.

4.   You must turn on the _____ before you make a turn.

5.   Open the _____ to check the oil.

6.   Many people prefer an automatic car to a car with a _____.

7.   You should put your packages in the _____ of your car.

8.   Step on the _____ to stop your car.

9.   Press the _____ to warn someone that you're coming.

10.   Most of the time, you should drive with two hands on the _____.

LEISURE ACTIVITIES

AT WORK Ask and answer questions about a person's job

ACADEMIC Take notes on information you hear; recognize and use different forms of words; identify and use transition words to organize writing; create and interpret bar graphs

CIVICS Research and report key information about a city; identify neighborhood benefits of community gardens

A man plays an unusual game of chess in Union Square Park, New York City.

Look at the pictures and label the leisure activities.

cards	dominoes	photography	traveling
cooking	fishing	sewing	video games
dancing	gardening	softball	yoga

1. _____dominoes_____

4. _____

7. _____

10. _____

2. _____

5. _____

8. _____

11. _____

3. _____

6. _____

9. _____

12. _____

B **LET'S TALK.** Which activities in Exercise A do you like to do? What other activities do you enjoy? Discuss your choices with a partner.

WORD PARTNERSHIPS	
play	dominoes
	softball
	cards
	video games
go	dancing
	fishing
do	yoga

A **ACADEMIC** Review *Yes / No* questions in Appendix A. Then, complete the questions. Use the activities from the previous page.

Noun	Verb
cooking	to cook
gardening	to garden
photography	to take photos
sewing	to sew
traveling	to travel

1. Are you going to _____travel_____ this weekend?
2. Are you going to _____ next month?
3. Were you _____ last weekend?
4. Were you _____ last month?
5. Do you like to _____?
6. Do you _____ every day?
7. Did you _____?
8. Did you _____ yesterday?
9. Will you _____ next weekend?
10. Are you _____ right now?

B **LET'S TALK.** With a partner, ask and answer the questions in Exercise A.

C **LET'S TALK.** With a partner, ask and answer *Yes / No* questions about the pictures. Use your imagination and the time expressions below.

every day	last Friday	next weekend	right now	tomorrow	yesterday

Men play dominoes in the Little Havana neighborhood of Miami.

> Do they play dominoes every day?

> No, they don't. They only play on Fridays.

Tao Porchon-Lynch is the world's oldest yoga instructor at 99 years old.

> Is she doing yoga right now?

> Yes, she is.

ACTIVE GRAMMAR | Questions with *Who* and *Whose*

Whose umbrella is that?	It's mine.
Who likes sports?	I do.
Who do you cook for?	I cook for my friends.

Whose asks questions about possession.
    Whose pencil is this?
Who asks questions about the subject or object.
    Who dances on Saturdays?
    Who do you dance with?

A People are talking about activities they enjoy. Circle the correct question words. Then, listen and answer the questions. 🎧 24

Carla

Roberta

Yelena

1. **Who** / **Whose** likes to go dancing?   *Carla does*_____.

2. **Who** / **Whose** father taught her chess? _____.

3. **Who** / **Whose** has many books about her hobby? _____.

4. **Who** / **Whose** does Carla go dancing with? _____.

5. **Who** / **Whose** friends often meet at dance clubs? _____.

6. **Who** / **Whose** does Roberta meet once a month? _____.

7. **Who** / **Whose** gets information on social media? _____.

8. **Who** / **Whose** has more free time now? _____.

B Work in groups. Write *Who* or *Whose* for each question. Then, ask and answer the questions.

1. _____*Who*_____ has a hobby?

2. _____ family has a garden?

3. _____ family is planning a trip?

4. _____ exercises regularly?

5. _____ has a pet?

6. _____ mother or father likes to cook?

Present	Subject	Who **goes** to the gym every day?	<u>Beth</u> does.
	Object	Who **does** Beth **go** to the gym with?	She goes <u>with her sister</u>.
Past	Subject	Who **went** to the gym?	<u>Jim</u> did.
	Object	Who **did** Jim **go** to the gym with?	He went <u>with his wife</u>.

A Complete the questions about the women's weekend activities. Use the simple past or simple present.

Rosa

Melba

Paula

1. Who (take) _____*took*_____ a cooking class? Rosa did.
2. Who (Rosa / take) _____*does / did Rosa take*_____ the class with? With two other students
3. Who (enjoy) _____ the food Rosa makes? Her husband does.
4. Who (play) _____ cards every Sunday? Melba does.
5. Who (Melba / play) _____ with? With her friends
6. Who (plant) _____ some flowers last weekend? Paula did.
7. Who (help) _____ Paula with the flowers? No one did.
8. Who (Paula / get) _____ advice from? From a gardening club

B **LET'S TALK.** Complete the questions about your classmates. Use the simple past or simple present. Then, ask and answer the questions with a partner.

1. Who usually (arrive) _____*arrives*_____ late to class?
2. Who (sit) _____ next to you every day?
3. Who (work) _____ full time?
4. Who (you / text) _____ before class?
5. Who (wear) _____ glasses?
6. Who (you / come) _____ to school with today?
7. Who (arrive) _____ early this morning?

How do you get to work?	I take <u>the bus</u>.
How far do you live from school?	I live about <u>three miles</u> away.
How long did you wait?	I waited <u>30 minutes</u>.
How much money do you have?	I have <u>$4.00</u>.
How many tickets do you have?	I only have <u>two</u>.
How often do you come to school?	I come to school <u>three days a week</u>.

A Complete the questions with the correct *How* expression. Then, ask and answer the questions with a partner.

1. _____*How often*_____ do you visit your native country?

2. _____ siblings do you have?

3. _____ do you spend on transportation to school?

4. _____ are you going to live in this country?

5. _____ hours do you sleep each night?

6. _____ do you live from your job?

7. _____ did you find out about this school?

8. _____ do you go to the movies?

9. _____ did it take you to get to class today?

10. _____ is it from your home to school?

B **AT WORK** **LET'S TALK.** Ask your teacher these questions.

1. How did you find this teaching job?
2. How do you get to work?
3. How many students do you have?
4. How often do you give tests?
5. How many days a week do you work?
6. How far do you live from your job?

C **AT WORK** Write three more questions with *How* to ask about your teacher's job.

1. _____

2. _____

3. _____

Simple Present of *be*	You **are** from Thailand,	**aren't** you?
	It **isn't** cold today,	**is** it?
Present continuous	They **are having** a nice time,	**aren't** they?
	They **aren't having** a bad time,	**are** they?
Simple present	He **plays** soccer every day,	**doesn't** he?
	He **doesn't play** tennis,	**does** he?
Simple Past of *be*	They **were** at the park,	**weren't** they?
	They **weren't** at home,	**were** they?
Simple past	You **took** some pictures,	**didn't** you?
	You **didn't take** these pictures,	**did** you?
Future with *will*	She **will plant** more roses,	**won't** she?
	She **won't plant** any flowers,	**will** she?

We can use tag questions to confirm or express uncertainty about a statement.

Use falling intonation to confirm information.

> They play dominoes on Fridays, **don't they**?

Use rising intonation to express uncertainty.

> She doesn't like fishing, **does she**?

A **Pronunciation: Tag Questions** Listen and repeat. Then, listen again and draw arrows above the tag questions to show whether the intonation is rising or falling. 🎧 25

1. They like to fish, don't they?

2. Fishing isn't expensive, is it?

3. They'll cook their fish, won't they?

4. They don't fish every day, do they?

5. They're fishing in a lake, aren't they?

6. It isn't a hot day, is it?

7. Fishing isn't tiring, is it?

8. They hope to catch a lot, don't they?

B Write the correct tag questions. Ask and answer the questions with a partner. Pay attention to the intonation.

1. You are studying English, _____ *aren't you* _____?

2. You will be in class tomorrow, _____?

3. You were here yesterday, _____?

4. We won't have a test tomorrow, _____?

5. You have a car, _____?

6. It wasn't raining yesterday morning, _____?

7. You didn't come to class late today, _____?

A STUDENT TO STUDENT

Student 1: Turn to Appendix C. Read the **Set A** questions to Student 2.

Student 2: Listen to Student 1 and write the questions.

1. _____?

   My father did, and I also took classes.

2. _____?

   I took Indian cooking, candy-making, and barbecue, to name a few.

3. _____?

   Yes, I regularly watch cooking shows on television.

4. _____?

   It is now! We remodeled it a few years ago.

5. _____?

   I'm going to cook spaghetti with meatballs. I love Italian food.

Student 2: Turn to Appendix C. Read the **Set B** questions to Student 1.

Student 1: Listen to Student 2 and write the questions.

6. _____?

   Yes, sometimes. He took a couple of classes with me.

7. _____?

   We took a Valentine's Day class and a Mexican cooking class.

8. _____?

   I cooked oatmeal, but it was terrible!

9. _____?

   My husband and I are going to cook together!

10. _____?

   Because my job wasn't fun anymore, and I love to cook.

B Read. Then, complete the questions.

There are six people in the Yang family. They live in San Francisco, but they are originally from Hong Kong. They moved to San Francisco three years ago and lived with relatives until they found jobs. The parents, William and Patricia, spoke English fluently when they arrived, so they found work quickly. They work at the same hospital. William is an accountant in the billing department, and Patricia is a pediatric nurse. Their two oldest children, Charles and Margaret, are now college students. Charles is a medical student, and Margaret is studying architecture. Their youngest, Harry, is a high school student. The children are doing well in school. Grandmother Yang speaks English, too, and she volunteers in a library in Chinatown. The Yangs love to travel. This summer they are going to Vancouver, Canada to visit William's brother, Victor.

1. How many _people are in the Yang family_____?

   Six.

2. When _____?

   Three years ago.

3. Who _____?

   With relatives.

4. Why _____?

   Because they spoke English fluently.

5. How many _____?

   Three.

6. How _____?

   They're doing well.

7. Do _____?

   Yes, they do.

8. Whose _____?

   William's brother.

C Write two questions with *Who* about the Yang family. Ask a partner your questions.

1. Who _____?

2. Who did _____?

A Look at the pictures of different places in Vancouver. What might the Yangs do in each place? Use your imagination.

Capilano Suspension Bridge

Granville Island

Gastown

Queen Elizabeth Park

Vancouver Aquarium

Chinatown

B **ACADEMIC** Listen and take notes. 26

Victor	Lin	Yesterday / This morning	Later
-visited Vancouver on business			

C Listen again. Circle *True* or *False*. 🎧26

1. The Yangs are staying in a hotel.   True   (False)
2. Victor and his family moved to Vancouver five years ago.   True   False
3. Lin likes Vancouver now.   True   False
4. Lin works part time.   True   False
5. Lin can speak both Cantonese and Mandarin.   True   False
6. They had breakfast at a hotel restaurant.   True   False
7. They are going to see fish and other animals this afternoon.   True   False

D Match.

___d___ **1.** What did Victor like about Vancouver?   **a.** No, she didn't.

_____ **2.** Did Lin want to come to Vancouver at first?   **b.** In Queen Elizabeth Park

_____ **3.** How often does Lin work?   **c.** Next year

_____ **4.** Where did they go this morning?   **d.** The economic opportunities

_____ **5.** Where are they going to have dinner?   **e.** To Granville Island

_____ **6.** Where can they see a rose garden?   **f.** Three days a week

_____ **7.** When will Victor and his family go to San Francisco?   **g.** In Chinatown

E   **CIVICS**   Go online. Search for information on another Canadian city. Find three activities to do there and write sentences about them. Report to your classmates.

1. _____

2. _____

3. _____

Vancouver is the third largest city in Canada.

A Discuss the questions. Then, read the text.

1. Read the title of the text below. What does it mean?

2. Imagine you have a garden. What would you like to grow?

Community Gardening

In January, seed catalogs begin to arrive at homes across the United States. Hardware stores start selling seeds and plants. Gardening is a very popular hobby in this country. For some people, it is not just a relaxing activity, but also an economic bonus.

In many cities throughout the United States, there are community garden programs. According to the American Community Gardening Association, a community garden is "any piece of land gardened by a group of people." **Residents** who do not have yards where they can start gardens can grow vegetables and flowers in parks, on **vacant** city lots, or in other empty spaces in their neighborhoods. However, residents might need permission to start a garden on city property.

Among the **benefits** of community gardening are the **beautification** of neighborhoods, the social **interaction** between neighbors in the gardens, and the ability of families to save money on produce.

The gardens are usually organized by community members, and they help other residents select tools, seeds, plants, and other materials. Sometimes there is a children's program, which uses the gardens to teach elementary school students about science and math. Youth can also participate by helping with the gardening or giving tours to people who visit the gardens. Gardening can teach residents about healthy food, too. As you can see, a community garden does more than just grow fruits, flowers, and vegetables. 🎧 27

Ron Finley, nicknamed the "Gangsta Gardener," helps communities in South Central Los Angeles grow fruits, vegetables, and flowers along sidewalks and in vacant lots.

B **CIVICS** Circle *True* or *False*.

1.	Some people start gardens in order to save money.	(True)	False
2.	Residents can make gardens anywhere they want to.	True	False
3.	All gardeners put their gardens on private property.	True	False
4.	Every city has community gardens.	True	False
5.	Teenagers can help in the gardens.	True	False
6.	Gardening can help children learn science and math.	True	False
7.	Community garden programs have many purposes.	True	False

READING NOTE

Word Forms

Many words have different forms for different parts of speech including nouns, verbs, adjectives and others. When using a dictionary or translator, check that you are using the correct form of a word.

C **ACADEMIC** Read the word forms. Then, complete the sentences.

Noun	Verb	Adjective
beautification	beautify	beautiful
benefit(s)	benefit	beneficial
interaction(s)	interact	interactive
resident(s)	reside	residential
vacancy(ies)	vacate	vacant

1. In my city, there is a _____*beautiful*_____ community garden on my block.

2. There was a _____ in my building, so I told one of my friends who was looking for an apartment.

3. The people who work in the garden enjoy the social _____.

4. Only people who _____ in my neighborhood can use our garden.

5. There are many _____ to gardening.

D ▶**WATCH** Watch the video. Discuss the questions in groups.

1. Where have people created gardens in the video?

2. What benefits of urban gardening does the video mention?

A Read.

Linda Torres

October 25

How to Start a Garden

My husband and I enjoy gardening. We both had gardens in our old village, and now we have a garden at our new home. We like to grow vegetables, fruits, and flowers, so we always have enough to share with our friends, family, and neighbors. It is not difficult to start a garden, but it takes regular care and patience.

First, find a sunny spot in your yard. Try to find a place that gets sun all day long. Second, clear out the grass and large rocks in the space. Third, turn over the dirt, and add some compost to make the dirt better for growing fruits and vegetables. You can buy compost in a gardening store. After that, plan your garden. Decide what you want to grow and where you want to put different plants. Next, buy the seeds and/or small plants. Plant your seeds and plants according to the instructions on the packets or boxes. Then, cover the ground with mulch to keep down the weeds. We use old newspaper and leaves, but some people use straw or bags of mulch from a store. Finally, water your seeds and plants regularly, and don't forget to weed your garden. After some time, you'll have delicious, healthy fruits and vegetables for your family.

WRITING NOTE

Transition Words Review

You already know how to use transition words to explain a future plan. You can also use transition words to describe a process or to give instructions.

First, put the flour, sugar, and baking soda in a bowl. **Then**, add the cooking oil, eggs, and milk.

Gardening can be a good form of exercise and can relieve stress.

B Underline the transition words in the text in Exercise A.

| after that | finally | first | next | second | then | third |

C ACADEMIC Read about how to plant flowers. With a partner, number the sentences in the correct order. Then, rewrite the sentences in paragraph form in your notebook. Use the transition words from Exercise B.

_____ Add some fertilizer to the bottom of the hole.

_____ Water the flowers regularly.

_____ Dig a hole deep enough for the roots of your flowers.

___1___ Planting flowers is easier than planting seeds, but there are still some steps you need to follow.

_____ Buy flowers that will fit in the space you have. Read the tag to make sure the type of flower is right for your garden.

_____ Remove weeds from around the flowers.

___5___ Pull the flowers out of their container and break up the roots with your hands.

_____ Put the flowers in the hole and fill in the hole with dirt.

D ACADEMIC In your notebook, write a paragraph about a process that is related to one of your hobbies or interests. Give instructions on the steps of this process. Use transition words.

E ACADEMIC Read a classmate's paragraph. How many steps are there? Number the start of each step. Underline each transition word.

F Find and correct the mistakes.
1. What~~are~~ you doing?
2. Why does she has so many pets?
3. Where did you found those stamps?
4. How long will they plays this game?
5. You going to work in your garden?
6. Who did play a sport last weekend?
7. Who you go dancing with every Saturday?

A **ACADEMIC** Look at the graph. Work with a partner. Circle *True* or *False*.

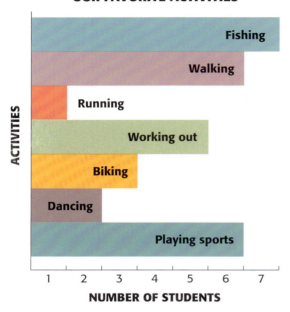

OUR FAVORITE ACTIVITIES

ACTIVITIES — Fishing, Walking, Running, Working out, Biking, Dancing, Playing sports

NUMBER OF STUDENTS — 1 2 3 4 5 6 7

1. Fishing is the most popular activity. (True) False

2. Biking is more popular than walking. True False

3. Walking is as popular as playing sports. True False

4. Working out at a gym is more popular than running. True False

5. Running is the least popular activity. True False

6. Dancing is more popular than biking. True False

B **ACADEMIC** **LET'S TALK.** Ask all of your classmates about their favorite activities and take notes. Write the five most popular activities on the lines on the left of the graph. Then, fill in the boxes to the right to show how many students like each activity.

OUR CLASS'S FAVORITE LEISURE ACTIVITIES

ACTIVITIES

NUMBER OF STUDENTS — 1 2 3 4 5 6 7 8 9 10 11 12 13 14 15 16

C **ACADEMIC** Answer the questions and complete the sentences about your graph.

1. Which activity is the most popular? _____

2. Which activity is the least popular? _____

3. _____ is more popular than _____.

4. _____ is less popular than _____.

AT WORK Identify appropriate responses to work-related situations; create and conduct a survey; report on the results of a survey

ACADEMIC Infer information from an image; scan a text and highlight important terms; use a graphic organizer to plan a piece of writing; categorize information in a chart

CIVICS Research and report key information about US landmarks

A man hikes one of the many mountains near Honolulu, Hawaii.

A **ACADEMIC** Work in groups. Discuss the places in the photos below. Then, write the name of each place under the correct photo.

Arches National Park	One World Trade Center	the Grand Canyon
~~Cape Canaveral~~	the Gateway Arch	the Space Needle
Niagara Falls	the Golden Gate Bridge	the Washington Monument

1. _____*Cape Canaveral*_____

4. _____

7. _____

2. _____

5. _____

8. _____

3. _____

6. _____

9. _____

B **CIVICS** **LET'S TALK.** Work with a partner. Do you know where each place is located? Go online to find the answers. Which of these places would you like to visit? Why?

I			
You			
We	**may**	**go** on vacation.	
They	**may not**	**need** a student visa.	
He	**might**		
She	**might not**		
It		**be** late.	

May (not) or *might (not)* can be used to express possibilities.

I **might go** on vacation.
(Meaning: Maybe I will go on vacation.)
He **may not need** a student visa.
(Meaning: Maybe he doesn't need a student visa.)

A Listen and complete the conversation. 🎧 28

A: Where are you planning to go on vacation this year?

B: My family and I are going to go to Washington, D.C.

A: That's nice! When are you going to go?

B: We _____ may go _____ at the end of March.

A: Are you going to fly?

B: No. That's too expensive. We _____ a bus, or we _____.

A: How long are you going to stay?

B: I don't have a lot of vacation time, so we _____ only a few days.

A: What are you going to do there?

B: Well, this will be our first trip to D.C. We _____ to a couple of museums.

A: That's a good idea. Many of the museums are free.

B: We _____ definitely _____ to the zoo.
My children are excited because they want to see the pandas.

A: Where are you going to stay?

B: We _____ with my brother, but he and his wife just had a baby.
They _____ space for us. We _____ with my aunt.

A: Are you going to see the cherry blossoms? I hear they're really beautiful.

B: Since we had such a hard winter, they _____ in bloom yet, but if they
are, I _____ a lot of pictures.

B Practice the conversation in Exercise A with a partner.

I You We They He She	might may	be	traveling. driving.
It			arriving late.

The present continuous form of *might* and *may* can be used to describe actions possibly occurring now or in the near future.

A: Why are they packing their car?
B: They **might be taking** a trip.

C Change each sentence. Use the present continuous form of *may* and *might*.

1. She might study French.

> She might be studying French.

2. They may take their dog to a friend's house.

3. He may shop for a new camera.

4. She might buy some gifts for her friends.

5. The students might prepare for their trip.

6. I might call my mother.

D Write a possible answer to each question. Use *may* or *might* in the simple present or present continuous forms.

1. Why isn't Anna in school?

   She might be sick.

2. Why is the flight late?

   _____

3. Why does Pedro always go to the mountains on vacation?

   _____

4. Why do they have to reschedule their trip?

   _____

5. Why are you packing a bottle of aspirin in your suitcase?

   _____

6. Why is Beth packing heavy sweaters for her beach vacation?

   _____

7. Why are they driving to Florida instead of flying?

   _____

ACTIVE GRAMMAR — *Must* for Inferences

I You We They He She	must	**have** the flu. **speak** French.
It		**be** cold.

Must can be used to make inferences. An inference is a guess about something that seems true.

Situation: Ann is walking outside in the winter. The temperature is 20° F, and Ann is wearing a T-shirt.

Inference: Ann **must be** cold.

More information in Appendix A.

A **ACADEMIC** **LET'S TALK.** With a partner, make inferences to answer the questions about the pictures. Use *must*.

> Where is he?

> He must be in New York City.

1. Where is he?

3. Why are they sleeping?

5. Why is she getting his autograph?

2. Where is she going?

4. Where is the traveler going?

6. Where are they?

B Listen. Write the number next to the correct response. 🎧 29

_____ **a.** You must be tired.

_____ **b.** You must be excited.

_____ **c.** He must be homesick.

_____ **d.** She must be nervous.

___1___ **e.** You must be relieved.

_____ **f.** You must be bored.

_____ **g.** She must be cold.

_____ **h.** You must be worried.

ACTIVE GRAMMAR / *Could* for Suggestions

You We They He She	**could**	**buy** tickets online. **bring** a backpack.

Could can be used to make suggestions.
    A: How should I get to the airport?
    B: You **could take** the shuttle.

A Listen and complete each suggestion. 🎧30

   1. You could *take the bus.* _____

   2. You _____

   3. _____

   4. _____

   5. _____

   6. _____

B **LET'S TALK.** Work with a partner. Take turns giving advice about the problems listed below. Use *could*.

> I want to go to Boston, but the hotels are very expensive.

> You could stay in a hostel. Hostels are cheaper than hotels.

   1. I want to go to Boston, but the hotels are very expensive.

   2. The bus to Los Angeles is cheap, but the traffic during rush hour is terrible.

   3. My husband / wife and I want to take a trip alone, but we have two young children.

   4. I'm flying to Chicago tomorrow night, but a big snow storm is coming tomorrow morning.

   5. I want to go swimming during my vacation, but I don't want to go to the beach.

   6. My brother is visiting Miami, but he doesn't know where to find a good restaurant for dinner.

   7. My sister wants to go on vacation somewhere with cold weather.

   8. I always visit family when I have vacation time. I want to travel somewhere new, but I don't want my family to feel bad.

ACTIVE GRAMMAR / *Would rather* and *Would prefer to*

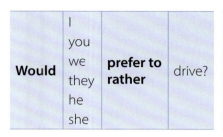

Would	I you we they he she	prefer to rather	drive?

I You We They He She	would 'd	prefer to rather	fly.

Would rather and *would prefer to* can be used to express preferences.

I'd rather go to New York than Miami.
I **would prefer to** drive.

A Ask and answer the questions with a partner. Give reasons for your answers.

> Would you rather fly or drive?   I'd rather fly. It's much faster.

1. Would you rather travel by bus or by train?
2. Would you prefer to check a bag or take a carry-on?
3. Would you rather go to the beach or to the mountains?
4. Would you prefer to go to a large city or to a small town?
5. Would you rather visit an art museum or a historical site?
6. Would you prefer to visit Tokyo, Japan or Barcelona, Spain?

B **AT WORK** **LET'S TALK.** In your notebook, write five questions with *would rather* and *would prefer to* to ask your classmates about their travel preferences. Walk around the class and ask five students your questions. Take notes. Then, report the results of one of your questions to the class.

> Would you rather travel in the morning or in the evening?

> I'd rather travel in the morning.

> Four students would prefer to travel in the morning, and one student would rather travel in the evening.

C **AT WORK** Write five sentences about your survey in your notebook.

Three students would rather travel in the spring than in the fall.

ACTIVE GRAMMAR | Modals Review

A **AT WORK** Match the workplace situations to the correct possibilities, inferences, or suggestions.

_____d_____ **1.** I don't feel well, and I have a big presentation tomorrow.

_____ **2.** Why isn't Patrick here?

_____ **3.** My coworker spilled coffee all over my new computer!

_____ **4.** My team has just completed a difficult project!

_____ **5.** It's boring to eat lunch at the company cafeteria.

_____ **6.** What's in the package?

_____ **7.** Where's our boss? She's never late.

_____ **8.** I worked until midnight last night.

a. You must be exhausted.

b. Would you rather go out to lunch with me?

c. It must be my office supplies. I ordered them last week.

d. You could email your boss.

e. He may not be coming into the office today.

f. You must be angry.

g. She might be stuck in traffic.

h. You must be pleased.

B **ACADEMIC** Write three sentences about each picture. Use *may, might, must, would rather,* or *would prefer to.*

1. The mother _____

_____.

2. The son _____

_____.

3. _____

_____.

4. He _____

_____.

5. The shoes _____

_____.

6. _____

_____.

C ACADEMIC STUDENT TO STUDENT

Student 1: Turn to Appendix C. Read the **Set A** sentences to Student 2. Then, listen to Student 2 and write each sentence next to the correct picture.

Student 2: Listen to Student 1 and write each sentence next to the correct picture. Then, turn to Appendix C and read the **Set B** sentences to Student 1.

1. _____
   _____.

2. _____
   _____.

3. _____
   _____.

4. _____
   _____.

5. _____
   _____.

6. _____
   _____.

THE BIG PICTURE | Planning a Vacation

A **ACADEMIC** Look at the picture and discuss the questions with a partner.

1. What do you see in the picture below? What are the people doing?

2. Where do you think this place is? Choose one of the states from the map.

3. Would you like to visit this place? Why?

A **lodge** is a type of resort hotel that is often located in the mountains.

B Listen and circle *True* or *False*. 🎧31

1.	The children will be out of school for a month.	True	~~False~~
2.	Gina will celebrate her birthday soon.	True	False
3.	Gina's sister visited Montana last summer.	True	False
4.	The lodge has a good view of the mountains.	True	False
5.	Both of their children are easy to please.	True	False
6.	Their daughter, Gabby, knows how to swim.	True	False
7.	Drew would rather swim in the lake than in a pool.	True	False
8.	The lodge doesn't offer any indoor sports.	True	False

C Listen again. Circle the activities that are available at the lodge. 🎧 31

basketball	lessons for sports	(swimming)
camping	movies	tennis
computer lessons	riding bicycles	transportation to town
games	skateboarding	volleyball

D Answer the questions.

1. What else can visitors do in the area?

   They can visit Glacier National Park. / They can go to town.

2. How far is the lodge from a major town?

   _____

3. How often do shuttles leave the lodge?

   _____

4. What can tourists do at the national park?

   _____

5. What are Gina and Drew going to do next?

   _____

E **Pronunciation: 'd rather / 'd prefer** Listen. Complete the sentences with *I'd, He'd, She'd,* *We'd,* or *They'd.* 🎧 32

1. ____*We'd*____ rather go to Montana.

2. _____ prefer to stay in a lodge.

3. _____ rather go fishing.

4. _____ prefer to go sailing.

5. _____ prefer not to swim in a lake.

6. _____ rather not go into town.

7. _____ prefer not to stay in a tent.

8. _____ rather not stay inside all day.

Mountain goats in Glacier National Park

READING | Travel Guide

A Discuss the questions.

1. Where is Argentina?

2. What do you know about Argentina?

B **ACADEMIC** Find and underline the words below in the reading. Then, match the words with their definitions.

<u>　d　</u> **1.** borders   **a.** an Argentine dance

_____ **2.** tango   **b.** amazing or unusual sights

_____ **3.** vibrant   **c.** a person who travels to find information

_____ **4.** wonders   **d.** touches another country or geographical feature

_____ **5.** explorer   **e.** lively; full of life and energy

C Read the text.

D Circle *True* or *False*.

1. Argentina borders Bolivia, Colombia, and Peru.	True	(False)
2. Buenos Aires is the largest city in South America.	True	False
3. Soccer is a popular sport in Argentina.	True	False
4. Buenos Aires has more than one art museum.	True	False
5. There are many places to shop for leather.	True	False
6. Buenos Aires is quieter than El Calafate.	True	False
7. Perito Moreno Glacier was named after an American.	True	False
8. Visitors can see the glaciers by boat.	True	False

Avenida 9 de Julio in Buenos Aires is often called the widest avenue in the world.

A Visit to Argentina

Argentina is located on the South American continent. It <u>borders</u> the South Atlantic Ocean, Chile, Uruguay, Paraguay, Bolivia, and Brazil. If you are looking for a place where you can experience both the life of vibrant cities and natural wonders, you might want to visit Argentina.

You could start your trip in the capital of Argentina, Buenos Aires. Buenos Aires is the largest city in Argentina and the second largest city in South America. It has one of the busiest ports in South America. After arriving at the international airport, it is an easy trip to a downtown hotel. The city has a variety of transportation, including trains, buses, and ferries. Visitors can spend time touring different neighborhoods, including Recoleta and La Boca, home to Boca Juniors, one of Argentina's famous soccer clubs. Also, it is easy to get to any of the museums, such as the Latin American Contemporary Art Museum or the National Museum of Fine Arts. If you'd prefer something different, you could go to the World Tango Museum, a museum devoted to Argentina's famous dance. In addition, there is a botanical garden, a zoo, and restaurants that serve delicious *asado*, Argentine barbecue. If you'd rather do some shopping, there are many stores and shopping malls where you can find leather items, such as handbags, wallets, or jackets. As you can see, visitors will not be bored in Buenos Aires.

If you would rather get away from the busy city, fly to El Calafate. This is the starting point for a visit to Patagonia, the region farthest south in Argentina and Chile. El Calafate is located on the southern shore of Lake Argentino, near Los Glaciares National Park. Here you can see one of the natural wonders of the world, the Perito Moreno Glacier, which was named after an Argentine explorer, Francisco Moreno. One of the best ways to see the glaciers is to take a boat ride on Lake Argentino. You will be able to sail among icebergs and may get closer to the Perito Moreno Glacier. Also, some lucky visitors might see the Upsala Glacier, the largest glacier in South America. It is a fantastic sight.

When you plan your next vacation, think about going to Argentina. It will satisfy your need for the action of a city and the beauty of nature. 🎧 33

Tourists explore the Perito Moreno Glacier.

A Read.

Mayumi Sato
March 22

My Dream Vacation

When I have free time and money, I want to take a dream vacation. I would like to visit four South American cities: Lima and Cuzco in Peru, Buenos Aires in Argentina, and Rio de Janeiro in Brazil. Before I start my vacation, I might take a Spanish or Portuguese course. I will ask some of my South American classmates to give me some advice. They might know when is the best time to visit.

First, I will go to Peru. I'd prefer to fly into the capital city, Lima. I may spend a few days visiting the museums and looking at the architecture. The restaurants must have fresh seafood because Lima is on the coast. After a few days, I want to go to Cuzco to see Machu Picchu. It must be one of the most interesting archaeological sites in the world. When I get back to Cuzco, I might buy some souvenirs for my family and friends.

Then, I will travel to Buenos Aires, Argentina. I am taking dance lessons now, so I might take a tango class in Buenos Aires because a friend told me that Buenos Aires is the home of the tango. Also, I want to visit a traditional ranch because they must have delicious Argentine barbecue.

Finally, I will fly to Rio de Janeiro, Brazil for my last stop. I may take a class at a samba school. The samba is a traditional Brazilian dance. I'd rather relax on the famous Copacabana Beach than see the museums, but I may do both! Rio de Janeiro must be a very exciting city. This will be a great vacation.

WRITING NOTE

Using a Graphic Organizer

It is important to plan before you write. Use a graphic organizer to help you plan your writing.

Inca rulers built Machu Picchu over 500 years ago.

B **ACADEMIC** Look at the graphic organizer. Read the plan for the text on the previous page.

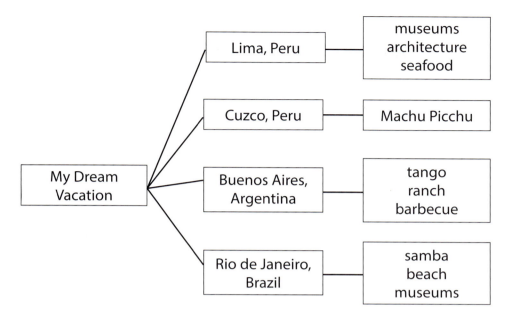

C **ACADEMIC** Use a graphic organizer to plan a text about your dream vacation. Answer the questions.

1. Where do you want to go? Why?

2. What time of year would you prefer to go there?

3. How long might you stay?

4. What might you do there?

D **ACADEMIC** Write about your dream vacation. Use the ideas from your graphic organizer.

E Read a partner's text. Answer the questions.

1. Where does your partner want to go on a dream vacation?

2. Why do they want to go there?

F Find and correct the modal verb mistakes.

1. I might ~~to~~ visit a museum.

2. He may not took a class this semester.

3. They might be look in his suitcase.

4. She could going by train.

5. We rather not use a credit card.

6. He must not has a passport.

7. You would rather fly today or tomorrow?

8. She must homesick.

A Listen and answer the questions. 🎧 34

1. Where did she go?
   (To) Barcelona and Madrid
2. Where did she stay?
3. Where was her luggage?

4. Did anyone ask her to carry anything in her bag?
5. Did the inspector open her bag?
6. What happened?

B ACADEMIC **LET'S TALK.** Work in a group. Read the lists below. Then:

1. Cross out items on the lists that are not allowed.
2. Move items from one list to the other when necessary.
3. Compare your lists with another group.

Items in Carry-on Bag	Items in Checked Bag
two paperback books	five shirts
a baseball glove	one pair of jeans
a cellphone	underwear and socks
a small bottle of aspirin	two baseball bats
~~a large bottle of shampoo~~	a jacket
a large bottle of suntan lotion	a US passport
an army knife	matches
a pair of shoes	a pair of dress shoes
a small can of shaving cream	two belts
fireworks	a bag of energy bars
	a large bottle of shampoo

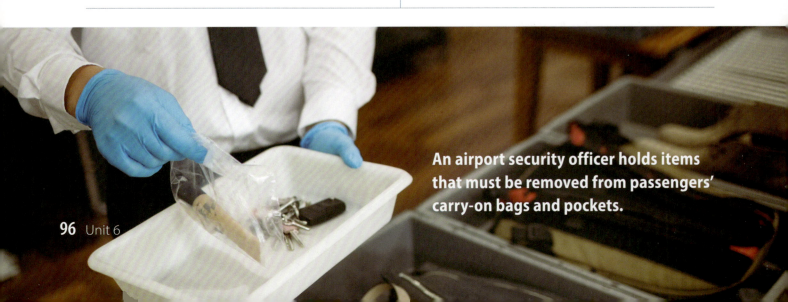

An airport security officer holds items that must be removed from passengers' carry-on bags and pockets.

UNIT 7 SPORTS

An ice sledge hockey match at the Paralympic Winter Games.

AT WORK Ask and answer questions about recent work activities; collect, record, and report information about classmates' work history

ACADEMIC Categorize information in a chart; formulate questions about a text; use conjunctions to combine sentences

CIVICS Identify terms for common injuries and their treatments

A Write the letter of each sentence next to the correct name.

> **a.** She has been playing doubles for many years.
> **b.** He has been trying to win the Super Bowl for a long time.
> **c.** She has been racing cars since she was a teenager.
> **d.** He has been talking to his fans for 20 minutes.
> **e.** He has been playing soccer for a Brazilian team for two years.
> **f.** She has been neglecting her schoolwork to play golf.

WORD PARTNERSHIPS	
female	
male	
high school	athlete
college	
amateur	
professional	

1.

____a____ Angelica Jones

4.

_____ Kristine Park

2.

_____ Melinda Gomez

5.

_____ Dave Meese

3.

_____ Marco Ronaldo

6.

_____ Alfredo Perez

Present Perfect Continuous

| I
You
We
They | **have**
've | **been** | play**ing** tennis for two hours.
watch**ing** baseball since 1:00 p.m.
work**ing** all day. |
| He
She | **has**
's | | |

We can use the present perfect continuous to describe an action that began in the past and is continuing now or has recently ended.
I **have been** swimm**ing** for an hour.

A Complete the sentences. Use the correct form of the verb.

1. It's 2:00.

   Carl _____ is playing _____ basketball.

   Carl (begin) _____ began _____ playing basketball at 1:00.

   He _____ 's / has been playing _____ basketball for an hour.

   He _____ 's / has been playing _____ basketball since 1:00.

2. It's 6:00.

   The men _____ soccer.

   They (start) _____ playing soccer at 4:00.

   They _____ soccer for two hours.

   They _____ since 4:00.

3. It's 12:00.

   The women _____ tennis.

   They (begin) _____ playing tennis at 10:00.

   They _____ tennis for two hours.

   They _____ tennis since 10:00.

4. I _____ English.

   I _____ studying English in _____.

   I _____ English for _____.

   I _____ English since _____.

B **Pronunciation: 've been / 's been** Listen and write. Then, listen and repeat. 🎧 35

1. _____ *She's* _____ been taking tennis lessons.

2. _____ been working hard.

3. _____ been playing baseball.

4. _____ been skateboarding.

5. _____ been kicking soccer balls.

6. _____ been training for a marathon.

7. _____ been learning to ice skate.

8. _____ been playing basketball.

C Listen to the conversation. Then, practice it with a partner. 🎧 36

A: Hi! What've you been up to?

B: I've been taking dance lessons.

A: Dance lessons? When did you start doing that?

B: My fiancée and I started a couple of weeks ago. We've been practicing for the wedding.

A: That's great. How's it going?

B: So far, it's been going well.

A: Glad to hear that! Good luck with your lessons.

B: Thanks!

D With a partner, write a new conversation using the present perfect continuous. Then, practice the conversation together.

A couple dances together during a tango lesson.

ACTIVE GRAMMAR / *For* and *Since*

For
For shows an amount of time.
I've been watching the game **for** a few minutes.
He's been training **for** three days.
They've been playing golf **for** ten years.

Since
Since shows when an action started.
I've been watching the game **since** 5:00.
He's been training **since** Monday.
They've been playing golf **since** they retired.

A **ACADEMIC** Write each word or phrase under *for* or *since*.

2:00	about two weeks	I was a child	several days
a few minutes	he broke his arm	many years	she began to play tennis
a long time	he joined the team	Saturday	three hours

For	Since
a few minutes	2:00

B Complete the sentences. Use *for* or *since*.

1. She's been playing professionally _____for_____ five years.

2. He's been working out _____ 8:00 this morning.

3. The team has been practicing _____ about three hours.

4. She's been riding her bicycle _____ two hours.

5. The girls have been practicing their routine _____ 3:00.

6. The players have been listening to the coach _____ 30 minutes.

7. He hasn't been running well _____ he hurt his leg.

8. The fans have been buying snacks _____ they arrived at the stadium.

ACTIVE GRAMMAR | Present Perfect Continuous: *Yes / No* Questions

Have	I you we they	been	watching the game? playing on a team? working?
Has	he she		

Yes, you **have**.	No, you **haven't**.
Yes, I **have**.	No, I **haven't**.
Yes, we **have**.	No, we **haven't**.
Yes, they **have**.	No, they **haven't**.
Yes, he **has**.	No, he **hasn't**.
Yes, she **has**.	No, she **hasn't**.

A **AT WORK** With a partner, ask and answer questions using the words below and the present perfect continuous.

> Have you been studying hard?

> Yes, I have.

1. you / study / hard
2. you / work / overtime
3. you / look for / a new job
4. you / get / enough sleep
5. you / exercise

6. your classmates / speak / English in class
7. the teacher / give / a lot of homework
8. the teacher / give / quizzes
9. you / listen to / music in English
10. you / watch / TV in English

B **ACADEMIC** Read the paragraph. Then, complete the questions.

Daniel and Monica are professional skiers. Daniel has been skiing since he was a young child. Monica has been skiing since she was 14 years old. Daniel won three competitions last year. Monica won the national competition two months ago. Now, they're training for the Olympics. They've been training for a long time, but they've been training together for only a short time. It's been going well so far!

1. Has Daniel been skiing since he was a child _____? Yes, he has.

2. _____ since she was a child? No, she hasn't.

3. _____ last year? Yes, he did.

4. _____ two months ago? Yes, she did.

5. _____ for a long time? No, they haven't.

C STUDENT TO STUDENT

Student 1: Turn to Appendix C. Read the **Set A** sentences to Student 2. Then, listen to Student 2 and write each sentence next to the correct picture.

Student 2: Listen to Student 1 and write each sentence next to the correct picture. Then, turn to Appendix C and read the **Set B** sentences to Student 1.

1. _____

2. _____

3. _____

4. _____

5. _____

6. _____

7. _____

8. _____

ACTIVE GRAMMAR | Present Perfect Continuous: *How long* Questions

How long	have	I you we they	been	studying English? living here? working?
	has	he she		

How long can be used to ask about length of time.

I've been studying English for two months.

He**'s been living** here since 2017.

A **AT WORK** **LET'S TALK.** Work in a group with four or five students. Complete the questions. Then, ask and answer the questions and write the answers in the chart.

1. How long have you been living in the United States?

2. How long have you been studying English?

3. How long have you been working in the United States?

4. How long _____?

5. How long _____?

Names	Question 1	Question 2	Question 3	Question 4	Question 5
1.					
2.					
3.					
4.					
5.					

B Write sentences using the information from your chart.

Mei has been living in the United States since 2013 _____.

1. _____ has been studying English _____.

2. _____ has been _____.

3. _____.

4. _____.

5. _____.

C ACADEMIC Complete the questions. Then, listen and check what you wrote. 🎧 37

Does	How long	How often	How old	What	Who

1. _____*What*_____ did Robert win?
2. _____ is he?
3. _____ has he been playing tennis?
4. _____ taught him how to play?
5. _____ he take private lessons?
6. _____ has he been taking private lessons?
7. _____ do his parents want him to practice?

D Listen again. Then, ask and answer the questions in Exercise C with a partner. 🎧 37

E ACADEMIC Read the paragraph. Then, complete the questions using the correct verb form.

My name is Imani, and I've been playing basketball since I was seven years old. My grandmother gave me my first basketball and taught me how to play. From that time on, I've been playing every day. My high school team has won the state championship twice. This year, our team has been winning a lot, but we had our first loss last week. My parents have been attending all of my games, and my grandmother has, too. She usually sits behind our team's bench. We're getting ready to play now, and my grandmother has been cheering very loudly. She's one of our most loyal fans.

1. How long *has Imani been playing basketball* _____?
   Since she was seven

2. Who _____?
   Her grandmother did.

3. How often _____?
   Every day

4. Has _____?
   Yes, it has.

5. When _____?
   They had it last week.

6. Who _____?
   Her parents and her grandmother have.

7. Where _____?
   Behind the team's bench

8. Has _____?
   Yes, she has.

THE BIG PICTURE / A Soccer Game

A In each circle, write the number of the correct person or people from the box below.

1. announcer	**2.** coach	**3.** concession workers	**4.** fans	**5.** official	**6.** players

B Listen to the story. Then, answer the questions. 🎧 38

1. Is it the first half or the second half?
2. How many minutes are left in the game?
3. What's the score?
4. How many fans are at the game?
5. What have the concession workers been doing?
6. What have people been buying?
7. How long has the wait at the concession stand been?
8. Has there been any fighting on the field?
9. What has the Stars' coach been doing?
10. Who has everyone been watching?

C Complete the sentences. Use the correct verb from the box in the present perfect continuous.

| buy | describe | ~~make~~ | pull | run | support | wait | watch |

1. The fans _____ have been making _____ a lot of noise.

2. The fans _____ a lot of soda and water.

3. People _____ in line to buy food.

4. An announcer _____ the action on the field.

5. The players _____ up and down the field.

6. A few of the players _____ each other's shirts.

7. Everyone _____ Stars player number 7.

8. The fans _____ their favorite players.

D Match the questions with the answers.

__d__	**1.** Is the stadium full?	**a.**	Yes, there are.
____	**2.** Did the game start at 2:00?	**b.**	Yes, he has.
____	**3.** Are there more than 20,000 fans?	**c.**	Yes, he does.
____	**4.** Have the fans been cheering for their favorites?	**d.**	Yes, it is.
____	**5.** Are the fans hot?	**e.**	Yes, it did.
____	**6.** Has the Stars' coach been shouting?	**f.**	Yes, they are.
____	**7.** Do the Stars have four goals?	**g.**	No, it isn't.
____	**8.** Does Stars player number 7 have the ball?	**h.**	No, he hasn't.
____	**9.** Is the score 4–1?	**i.**	Yes, they have.
____	**10.** Has the official been giving any red cards?	**j.**	No, they don't.

E **ACADEMIC** **LET'S TALK.** Work with a partner. Ask and answer *Yes / No* questions about the story in Exercise B. Use the present perfect continuous.

> Have the fans been waving their banners?

> Yes, they have.

The World Cup

Soccer is the most popular sport in the world. In the United States, people call the sport "soccer," but in many other countries, people call it "football." Soccer is a popular sport for many reasons. One reason is that it doesn't require a lot of equipment or a specific field. People can play with just a ball and enough space to run. Another reason is that there are intense **rivalries** between some cities that have soccer teams. These rivalries increase interest in the sport, as more people watch the games to cheer for their cities' teams. Finally, the World Cup is an event that the world **looks forward to** watching every four years.

FIFA (Fédération Internationale de Football Association) was founded in Paris, France in 1904. At the 1908 Summer Olympics, soccer became an official Olympic sport, organized by FIFA. At that time, however, only amateur athletes participated, and in 1914, FIFA **recognized** the Olympic soccer tournament as an amateur event. The World Cup then became the event that included professionals.

Uruguay was the host of the first World Cup in 1930. Thirteen countries participated: seven from South America, four from Europe, and two from North America. Uruguay was the favorite because it had two Olympic wins, so it was not a surprise that Uruguay won the first World Cup. Other countries that hosted the World Cup in the early years were Italy, France, and Brazil. In 1942 and 1946, the World Cup did not happen because of World War II, but since 1946, FIFA has been holding the event every four years.

Today, going to a stadium is only one of the ways to watch a match. Recently, fans have been watching the World Cup and other soccer tournaments on many **platforms**. They have not only been watching on TVs and listening on radios, but also streaming matches through apps and websites on cellphones, tablets, computers, and even video game systems. This allows fans to watch or listen to almost any match, no matter where they live.

Even though soccer is not as popular among Americans as other sports, it has been getting more and more popular. One event that **sparked** American interest in soccer was the 1994 World Cup, which was held in the United States. Today, many young people play soccer throughout the US. With both men's and women's professional leagues, it is expected that the number of American soccer fans will continue to grow. 🎧 39

Local fans watch a World Cup soccer match on a beach in Rio de Janeiro, Brazil.

A Discuss the questions.

1. Do you like to watch the World Cup? Why?
2. Where is the next World Cup going to be held?

B Read the text. Then, match the words with the definitions.

___d___ **1.** look forward to   **a.** feelings of competition between people or groups

_____ **2.** recognize   **b.** create

_____ **3.** platforms   **c.** officially accept

_____ **4.** rivalries   **d.** be excited about something

_____ **5.** spark   **e.** types of technological systems

C Circle *True* or *False*.

1. Around the world, people call the sport "soccer."	True	(False)
2. Soccer does not require a lot of equipment.	True	False
3. The US organized the first Olympic soccer game.	True	False
4. Professionals did not play in the 1908 Olympics.	True	False
5. The first World Cup was held in Europe.	True	False
6. Fans can watch soccer in many different ways.	True	False

D Read each sentence. Circle the letter of the sentence that has a similar meaning.

1. The World Cup is an event that the world **looks forward to** watching.
   a. No one is interested in the World Cup.
   (b.) People around the world are interested in the World Cup.

2. FIFA **recognized** the Olympic soccer tournament as an amateur event.
   a. FIFA considered the Olympic tournament to be for amateurs only.
   b. FIFA understood that the Olympics were popular among fans.

3. One event that **sparked** American interest in soccer was the 1994 World Cup.
   a. The 1994 World Cup caused more Americans to think about soccer.
   b. Many Americans attended the fireworks at the World Cup in 1994.

E ▶ **WATCH** Watch the video and check the statements you hear. Then, discuss the statements you heard in groups.

☐ **1.** "Anybody can play it. All you need is just a ball."

☐ **2.** "This year, the World Cup is in the Middle East."

☐ **3.** "Soccer is a great way of intercultural exchange."

A Discuss the questions.

1. What is lacrosse?
2. Do people play lacrosse in your country?
3. What sports are the most popular in your country?

B Read.

Jie Lin
December 12

Lacrosse

Lacrosse is a sport that started with Native Americans. Young men played for recreation, for religious reasons, and in preparation for war. They played with a wooden ball, a stick, and a net. As in soccer, lacrosse players had to get the ball into a goal, but they used a stick to move the ball across the field. The rules were simple—they could not touch the ball with their hands.

A French missionary first saw a lacrosse match in the 1630s. He wrote about the game, and he named it "lacrosse." After that, interest in the sport gradually grew. In 1856, a Canadian dentist founded a lacrosse club, but he changed the number of players, added a rubber ball, and changed the stick. Lacrosse was played in the 1904 and 1908 Summer Olympics, and the Canadian team won both times. People from all over the world attended the games, so after that, lacrosse began spreading to other countries.

The popularity of lacrosse has been growing quickly. The number of high school and college programs has been increasing. Some of the strongest teams are in the eastern part of the United States, but many other countries around the world have also been starting lacrosse clubs.

WRITING NOTE

Two short sentences can be combined with conjunctions like *and*, *but*, and *so*. In this case, a comma is needed before the conjunction.

And can introduce extra information; *but* can introduce a contrast or something different; *so* can introduce a result.

He wrote about the game, **and** he named it "lacrosse."

As in soccer, the players had to get the ball into a goal, **but** they used a stick to move the ball.

People from all over the world attended the games, **so** after that, lacrosse began spreading to other countries.

C ACADEMIC In your notebook, combine the sentences with *and*, *so*, or *but*.

1. My sisters are going to arrive tomorrow. They will see my team play.
   My sisters are going to arrive tomorrow, so they will see my team play.
2. My team has been practicing every day. We're not getting any better.
3. Bill hasn't been attending soccer practice. He has missed a few games.
4. The women's team has been playing well. I think they're going to go to the finals.
5. Ben wanted to play baseball. He broke his hand during the first game.
6. Karin lifts weights three times a week. She runs in the park every morning.

D ACADEMIC In your notebook, write about a popular sport. Use information from the internet or from library books. Use the conjunctions *and*, *but*, and *so* in some of your sentences. Do not copy sentences; use your own words.

E Read your partner's text. Answer the questions.

1. Which sport did your partner write about? _____
2. What interesting fact did you learn about this sport? _____

F Find and correct the mistakes.

1. I been playing a lot of soccer this year. *'ve*
2. He has been show me how to play tennis.
3. She's been exercising since 30 minutes.
4. We have been playing well for September.
5. They have been live in Tampa for six months.
6. She been training for the Olympics.
7. You have been working out every day?
8. How long you been watching the game?

Soccer stadium in Gdansk, Poland

A **CIVICS** Listen and repeat. 🎧 40

1. I have a bruise.

3. She has a sprained ankle.

5. Her arm is sore.

2. He has a concussion.

4. He has a pulled muscle.

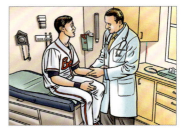

6. He has a broken wrist.

B **CIVICS** Listen. Take notes about each injury and its treatment. Then, compare your answers with a partner. 🎧 41

1. Injury: _a broken wrist_ _____

Treatment: _surgery and three months or more of recovery_ _____

2. Injury: _____

Treatment: _____

3. Injury: _____

Treatment: _____

4. Injury: _____

Treatment: _____

5. Injury: _____

Treatment: _____

6. Injury: _____

Treatment: _____

AT WORK Read about a promotion; recognize culturally appropriate messages for special occasions; create a greeting card for a classmate

ACADEMIC Categorize information in a chart; infer the meaning of new vocabulary; skim a text to find the main idea; use additional details to improve a text

CIVICS Read and understand descriptions of community service

Irving Kahn, who was the oldest living professional investor, celebrated his 106th birthday in 2011.

A Discuss the questions.

1. How many people are in your family?

2. How do you keep up-to-date on what is happening in your extended family?

3. What is a family reunion? Have you ever had one? If so, give some details.

B Listen. Clara and Gloria are talking about plans for a family reunion. Circle *True* or *False*. 🎧 42

1.	Clara and Gloria haven't spoken for a long time.	(True)	False
2.	The family had a reunion last year.	True	False
3.	Sara has decided on a date for the reunion.	True	False
4.	It's June now.	True	False
5.	They have emailed the invitations.	True	False
6.	Everyone's going to help with the food.	True	False
7.	There are 40 family members.	True	False
8.	Mateo has opened a small business.	True	False

Every five years, all members of the Servan-Schreiber family, ages nine months to 96, have a reunion.

I You We They	have / 've	**had** a dog **for** a long time.
	have not / **haven't**	**worked** there **for** two years.
He She	**has** / 's	**gotten** taller **since** January.
		been there **since** the company opened.
	has not / **hasn't**	

To form the present perfect simple, use *have / has* and the past participle.
The present perfect simple can be used:

- to describe an action that began in the past and is still true in the present.
  They **have lived** in the city **for** many years.
  She **hasn't seen** him **since** they broke up.
- to describe changes.
  He **has lost** over 50 pounds **since** he started exercising.
  In the past year, Lily **has grown** three inches.

More information in Appendix A.

A Underline the present perfect simple verbs. Circle *for* or *since* to make each sentence correct.

1. Clara and Gloria <u>haven't spoken</u> (**for**)/ **since** several months.

2. Tuan and Lana have been married **for / since** 1999.

3. Henry has belonged to the volunteer fire department **for / since** 2015.

4. Loanna has sold life insurance **for / since** six months.

5. Rita has been divorced **for / since** a year.

6. Richard has owned his own business **for / since** he moved to Ohio.

7. Tom has been in college **for / since** four years.

8. Anna has walked two miles a day **for / since** she had her heart attack.

9. Brian hasn't taken the bus **for / since** he got a new car.

10. We haven't seen our cat **for / since** a few days.

B Work with a partner. Use your imagination to complete the sentences. Use the simple past or the present perfect simple.

1. I haven't had a good night's sleep since _I had a baby_____.

2. I have had several complaints from my neighbors since _____
_____.

3. I have lost 10 pounds since _____.

4. I've made a few new friends since _____.

5. I haven't been able to concentrate on my job since _____
_____.

6. _____ since I fell in love.

7. _____ since I joined a gym.

8. _____ since I bought a dog.

9. _____ since I got a new job.

C Tim had a difficult first semester at college. Now, in his second semester, he has changed his habits. Turn to Appendix A and review the list of irregular past participles. Then, listen and complete the sentences. 🎧43

1. Tim _____ has become _____ a more serious student.

2. He _____ to improve his grades.

3. He _____ a tablet for his class notes.

4. He _____ all of his assignments.

5. He _____ behind in his work.

6. He _____ to his professors' office hours for extra help.

7. He _____ his homework in his room.

8. He _____ a tutor for help with chemistry.

9. He _____ more in class and participated in discussions.

10. He _____ out his cellphone to text during class.

11. His parents _____ very pleased with his progress.

Use the present perfect simple with words such as *just, lately,* and *recently* to describe an action in the recent past.

Put *just* between *have / has* and the main verb.

> I **have just quit** my job.

Lately is often placed at the end of a sentence.

> He **hasn't been** in class **lately**.

Recently is often placed between *have / has* and the main verb, or at the end of the sentence.

> They **have recently become** grandparents.
> They **have become** grandparents **recently**.

A Complete the sentences. Use the present perfect simple. Then, turn to Appendix A to check the irregular past participles you used.

1. I (just / meet) _____ *'ve / have just met* _____ Juan.

2. She (recently / fall) _____ in love.

3. He (just / spend) _____ $200 on textbooks.

4. Stanley (recently / get) _____ his driver's license.

5. Jing (not / see) _____ any new movies lately.

6. Ted and his family (just / move) _____ into a new home.

7. My sister (just / come) _____ home from Japan.

8. I (recently / find) _____ a new job.

9. My uncle (not / visit) _____ us lately.

10. My aunt (not / bring) _____ us any cakes lately.

B In your notebook, write two sentences about each picture. Use *just* in one sentence and *recently* in the other sentence.

Marco and Bianca

Marco

Bianca

C **Pronunciation: Stress for Clarification** Listen to the stress as each speaker clarifies the information. Underline the stressed word in each conversation. 🎧 44

1. **A:** I hear that David has recently lost his job.

   B: Not at all. He's <u>quit</u> his job to start his own company.

2. **A:** I hear that Amy has just moved to North Carolina.

   B: Close. She's moved to South Carolina.

3. **A:** I hear that Nora has just gotten her driver's license.

   B: No, just the opposite. She's lost her driver's license!

4. **A:** I hear that Joe and Tom have just opened an Italian restaurant.

   B: Not Italian. They've opened a Mexican restaurant.

> **Stress**
>
> When a word is stressed, the word is said a little more loudly and clearly than the other words in the sentence. This gives more importance to the word.

D Practice the conversations above with a partner. Stress the underlined words. Then, use the words in parentheses below to complete the conversations and practice them with your partner.

1. **A:** I hear that Paul has just joined the baseball team.

   B: No, he's (quit) _____.

2. **A:** I hear that Alex and Kathy have just gotten a cat.

   B: Not exactly. (a dog) _____.

E **LET'S TALK.** Look at the pictures. In groups, describe four changes in these people's lives. Use the present perfect simple.

1.

Allen ten years ago

Allen today

2.

Mary and Tom five years ago

Mary and Tom today

ACTIVE GRAMMAR — *Already* and *Yet*

Already can show that an action is completed. *Already* is often used in affirmative sentences. You can use the present perfect simple or the simple past with *already*. The simple past is more often used with *already* in spoken English than in writing.

She **has already bought** the invitations.   She **already bought** the invitations.

Already is usually placed between *have / has* and the main verb, or at the end of the sentence.

She **has already bought** the invitations.   She **has bought** the invitations **already**.

Yet can show that an action has not been completed. *Yet* is often used at the end of questions and negative sentences. You can use the present perfect simple or the simple past with *yet*.

Has she **sent** the invitations **yet**?   **Did** she **send** the invitations **yet**?

She **hasn't sent** the invitations **yet**.   She **didn't send** the invitations **yet**.

A **ACADEMIC** Sara is planning a family reunion. Listen and check the things that have and have not been completed. 🎧 **45**

Completed	Not completed	Things to do for the reunion
✔		form a committee to help plan the reunion
		set a date
		design the invitations
		send the invitations
		find the email addresses of all the family members
		plan the activities and games
		plan the menu
		order the cake
		buy some decorations
		hire staff to help set up, serve food, and clean up
		gather photos for the party

B **LET'S TALK.** With a partner, use the present perfect simple to discuss Sara's to-do list. *Use already or yet.*

> She has already formed a committee to help plan the reunion.

> They haven't sent the invitations yet.

C LET'S TALK. George and Monica have just had a party. With a partner, talk about what they have and haven't done. Use the phrases in the box and *already* or *yet*.

blow out the candles	put away the food
clear off the table	sweep the floor
collect the cans and bottles	take down the decorations
eat the last piece of cake	turn off the music
empty the garbage can	wash the dishes
go to bed	

sweep – swept – swept
blow – blew – blown

> George and Monica have already turned off the music.

> They haven't washed the dishes yet.

D LET'S TALK. Ask a partner about what they have done today. Use the phrases below and *yet*.

check your email	eat something healthy	make your bed
do the dishes	get some exercise	take a quiz
do your homework	go to work	watch TV
eat lunch	make a presentation	

> Have you checked your email yet today?

> Yes, I have. I checked it early this morning.

The present perfect simple can be used to describe actions that began in the past and are true in the present. The present perfect simple can also describe events in the recent past.

I **have been** in this country for three years.

They **have just won** the lottery.

The present perfect continuous can be used to describe actions that began in the past and are continuing now or have recently ended.

We **have been working** at the restaurant since we moved here.

The simple past can be used to describe actions that were completed in the past.

She **graduated** from college in 2016.

They **moved** to New Mexico two years ago.

A Complete the sentences. Use the correct forms of the verbs in parentheses.

1. Dave (move) _____ *moved* _____ into his apartment one year ago.

   He (live) _____ *'s / has been living / has lived* _____ in his apartment for a year.

   The landlord (just / increase) _____ his rent by $200!

2. My mother and father (be married) _____ for a long

   time. They (get) _____ married in 1970.

3. I (begin) _____ working here in 2010. I (work)

   _____ here for a long time.

4. I (take) _____ my exam two weeks ago,

   but my professor (not / give) _____ me my grade yet.

5. Rachel (look) _____ for a new job for several months.

   She (quit) _____ her job four months ago.

6. Nick (lose) _____ 15 pounds since he started

   his diet. He (start) _____ his diet two months ago.

7. George (buy) _____ his convertible in 1992. He (drive)

   _____ it for over 25 years!

8. Luis and Amanda (just / move) _____ again. They (live)

   _____ in three countries since they joined the military.

THE BIG PICTURE Gossip

A ACADEMIC Discuss the words.

> broken off   convertible   gossip   grounded   promoted

B Listen. Write each person's name under the correct picture. 🎧 46

> Amy   ~~Diana~~   Grandpa Joe   Mary   Paul   Rosa

1. _____

3. _____

5. _____

2. _____ Diana

4. _____

6. _____

C Answer the questions.

1. Who has lied to her boss? Rosa
2. Who has just been promoted?
3. Who has just lost her job?
4. Who has recently broken off her engagement?
5. Who has decided to travel across the country?
6. Who has been grounded?

D Circle *True* or *False*.

1. Diana has fallen in love with her neighbor.   (True)   False
2. Diana still has Chris's ring.   True   False
3. Rosa told her boss that she was sick.   True   False
4. This is the first time that Amy has gotten in trouble.   True   False
5. Amy's parents have taken away her cellphone.   True   False
6. Paul has been promoted.   True   False
7. Paul has the best sales record in the company.   True   False
8. Mary got a new job as a security guard.   True   False
9. Grandpa Joe has bought a new car.   True   False
10. Grandpa Joe has dyed his hair gray.   True   False

E **Pronunciation: Surprise Intonation** Listen and repeat. 🎧 47

1. **A:** He bought a new convertible.   **B:** A new convertible?
2. **A:** He left yesterday.   **B:** He left?
3. **A:** I've just been promoted.   **B:** Promoted?
4. **A:** She's lost her job.   **B:** Lost her job?
5. **A:** They're engaged.   **B:** Engaged?
6. **A:** We're moving.   **B:** You're moving?

F Write three statements with surprising news in your notebook. Then, tell your partner the news. Your partner will respond with surprised intonation.

My brother went bungee jumping.

Bungee jumping?!

Bungee jumping is an extreme sport invented in New Zealand.

A Discuss the questions.

1. What is a newsletter?
2. Do you receive any newsletters? What are they about?
3. Do you have a family newsletter?
4. Why do some families have newsletters?

B **ACADEMIC** Skim the first three paragraphs of the newsletter on the following page. Write the main idea of each paragraph below.

Paragraph 1: _Plans for the family reunion_

Paragraph 2: _____

Paragraph 3: _____

> **READING NOTE**
>
> **Skimming for the Main Idea**
> Each paragraph has a main idea or topic. If you are trying to understand the main idea of a text, it can be helpful to skim the first few sentences of each paragraph.

C **ACADEMIC** Match the words with their meanings.

__d__ **1.** take on	**a.**	contribute money or time
_____ **2.** hassle-free	**b.**	became
_____ **3.** school board	**c.**	possibilities
_____ **4.** turned	**d.**	agree to do or have
_____ **5.** chip in	**e.**	in the future
_____ **6.** ahead	**f.**	easy
_____ **7.** leads	**g.**	a group who governs local schools

D **CIVICS** Read the newsletter about a fictional family on the following page. Then, work with a partner and answer the questions.

1. What are the dates of the family reunion? _The weekend of August 14_
2. Where is the barbecue on Saturday?
3. What was Alba's college major?
4. How old is Grandma Silvia going to be on her next birthday?
5. How has Frank gotten involved in his new community?
6. What does Ana do for her volunteer work?
7. Why has Frank decided not to run for the school board?
8. What happened to John?
9. Why does Carolina need a new job?

The Navarros in the News

Circle the weekend of August 14th in your calendars! This year's reunion committee includes Sara, Doris, Frank, and Luisa. For Saturday, we've already reserved a space at the Park Resort Hotel. The barbecue is going to be on the lawn by the pool. We'll all **chip in** for the food. We've also reserved a block of rooms for the weekend for anyone who wants to stay overnight. Contact Luisa at 555-2422 to reserve a room. People have requested a relaxing, **hassle-free** day on Sunday. We're talking to the resort caterer about a picnic lunch. Look for more details in next month's issue! Email your suggestions and comments to the committee members, or call Sara at 555-6739.

Congratulations to Alba Navarro! After five years of college, sometimes full time, sometimes part time, Alba has just graduated with a degree in social work. She has accepted a position at Atlantic Community Services, where she will be working with teens.

Grandma Silvia Navarro **turned** 99 on May 2nd. She has moved in with her daughter, Isabella, and son-in-law, Brad. Silvia enjoys TV, her flower garden, and visits from her four children, twelve grandchildren, and 30 great-grandchildren. She will become a great-great-grandmother in September! Silvia says that she is looking forward to her 100th birthday. She tells her children, "I'd like a big party!"

A Note from Frank and Ana:

Hi Everyone!

We moved to Florida about a year ago, and we've stayed very active. Ana and I have gotten involved in the community. I was a high school principal and teacher for many years, so I've started volunteering at the local high school. I began by tutoring biology. Then, the school asked me to help out in the office. Now, I volunteer there about three times a week! Ana has been tutoring some of the immigrant students in English. We've both enjoyed our volunteer work. A few weeks ago, someone asked me to join the **school board**. I thought about it, but I've just decided not to join. I'm retired! I enjoy volunteering, but I don't want to **take on** more responsibility. Ana and I have been playing tennis and riding our bikes regularly to help us stay in shape. If you want to come for a visit, email us. Our guest room is waiting for you!

Send your get-well cards to John. His knee replacement went well, but he has several weeks of physical therapy **ahead**.

Carolina is looking for job **leads**. Her company closed, leaving 75 accountants looking for work. If you have any suggestions, please email her. 🎧 48

A **AT WORK** Read the paragraph from a fictional family newsletter.

Lena Thompson

June 4

The Thompson Family Newsletter

My cousin Henry has just accepted a position as distribution manager at Davis and Bates. Davis and Bates is a growing furniture manufacturer in Sacramento, California. Henry will coordinate all the company's deliveries. The company has been operating with just 25 employees in its distribution center. They are planning to expand to 50 employees, so Henry has a difficult job ahead of him! Henry has already sold his house, and he will leave for Sacramento next month. Henry, his wife, Paula, and their two children have been staying with Paula's parents. Paula and the children will move to Sacramento after the family finds a new house there. Henry and his family are excited for this change, but they are also sad to leave their friends and family in Houston.

Sacramento, CA

WRITING NOTE

Reporting the Facts

When reporting facts, it is important to include details. Additional details provide interesting and clear information.

B **ACADEMIC** Rewrite the statements to include more information. Use your imagination.

1. Thomas has recently graduated from college.
Thomas has recently graduated from the University of Maryland with a degree in biology.

_____

2. Randy and Lisa have just had a baby.

_____

_____

3. Linda has recently celebrated her birthday.

_____

_____

4. Tom was in a car accident.

_____

_____

5. Ken and Susan celebrated their wedding anniversary.

_____

_____

6. Karin and Ross have just bought a house.

_____

_____

C Check and discuss your answers in groups. Has anyone in your extended family recently . . . ?

☐ graduated	☐ celebrated a birthday	☐ lost a job
☐ gotten married	☐ celebrated an anniversary	☐ accepted a new job
☐ gotten engaged	☐ taken a vacation	☐ had an accident
☐ gotten divorced	☐ moved	☐ had an operation
☐ had a baby	☐ retired	☐ passed away (died)
☐ other _____		

D **ACADEMIC** Write a factual article about an event that recently happened in your family, your class, or your school. Include additional details.

E Exchange papers with a partner. What did your partner write about? Did they include additional details?

F Find and correct the mistakes.

1. She ~~have~~ _has_ just found a new job.

2. They haven't gotten married already.

3. They has just celebrated their tenth wedding anniversary.

4. Jason has come already home from the hospital.

5. They have live in the same house since 2010.

6. Olga has graduated from Florida International University last month.

7. Grandma Barnes pass away on June 15.

8. The whole family just has enjoyed a wonderful reunion.

CULTURE NOTE

In the United States, groups of coworkers, friends, and family members often send a greeting card signed by the whole group. They may send a card to someone who is retiring or leaving, to someone who is getting married or having a baby, or to someone who is in the hospital or has lost a loved one. Each person writes a brief message and signs the card.

A **AT WORK** Match each card message with the appropriate occasion.

_c_	**1.** a new baby	**a.**	Get well soon! We hope you have a speedy recovery!
____	**2.** retirement	**b.**	We're going to miss you. Good luck in your new place!
____	**3.** a wedding	**c.**	Welcome to parenthood! Diapers, diapers, and more diapers!
____	**4.** moving away	**d.**	We wish you joy in your new life together!
____	**5.** an illness	**e.**	Good luck! We envy you!
____	**6.** a death in the family	**f.**	We express our deepest sympathy in your time of loss.

B **AT WORK** **LET'S TALK.** Work in groups. Create a greeting card for a classmate who is moving away. Write messages on the outside and inside of the card. Then, everyone should sign the card.

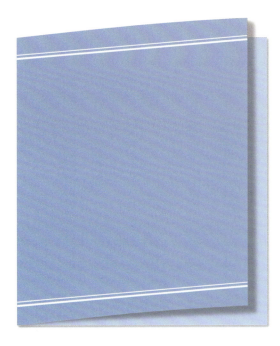

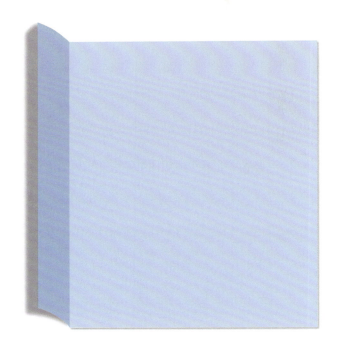

UNIT 9 JOB PERFORMANCE

AT WORK Identify job skills; ask and answer questions about work experiences; interpret job descriptions; recall information from a performance evaluation

ACADEMIC Differentiate between verb forms in sentences; recall key details from a text; identify definitions for terms in a text; cite sources using MLA format

CIVICS Assess personal job skills; research a job of interest

Blackstone Bicycle Works, a community bike shop in Chicago, provides on-the-job training to its employees in bicycle mechanics and repair, customer service, and management.

AT WORK With a partner, write the job under each photo. Then, discuss the questions.

1. Does this person work in production or service?
2. What skills does this person need for the job?
3. Would you like this kind of work? Why?

1. _____

4. _____

2. _____

5. _____

3. _____

6. _____

How long can ask about an amount of time. *How long* can be used with the present perfect continuous.

A: How long has she been repairing the TV?

B: She has been repairing it **for an hour**.

How many asks about a specific number. *How many* can be used with the present perfect simple.

A: How many TVs has she repaired this week?

B: She has repaired **three TVs** so far.

A Read the conversation. Then, practice it with a partner.

A: What is Harry doing?

B: He's registering students for classes.

A: How long has he been sitting at the registration counter?

B: He's been sitting there for two hours.

A: How many students has he registered so far?

B: He's registered 12 students so far today.

B **LET'S TALK.** With a partner, ask and answer questions about each picture using *How long* and *How many*. Use your imagination. Use Exercise A as an example.

1.

2.

3.

4.

5.

6.

The present perfect simple can be used to describe repeated past actions. *From time to time* and *a few times* are expressions that can show a repeated action. I have been late **from time to time.** She has worked overtime **a few times.**	*Ever* and *never* are often used with the present perfect simple. *Ever* means *at any time* and is often used in *Yes / No* questions or when comparing things. Have you **ever** been to France? This is the best job I've **ever** had. *Never* means *not at any time*. It is often used in statements, but it cannot be used with a negative verb. I have **never** worked at a school.

A **AT WORK** With a partner, ask and answer the questions. Use the present perfect simple and *from time to time, a few times,* or *never.*

> Have you ever called in sick?

> Yes, I've called in sick from time to time.

1. Have you ever called in sick?
2. Have you ever had an accident at work?
3. Have you ever quit a job?
4. Have you ever received a raise?
5. Have you ever gotten a promotion?
6. Have you ever received a performance evaluation?
7. Have you ever complained to your boss?
8. Have you ever complained about your boss?
9. Have you ever worked a double shift?
10. Have you ever had a problem with a coworker?

B **AT WORK** **LET'S TALK.** Ask your partner two more questions about work. Use the present perfect simple and *ever.*

C Make questions to ask your teacher using the present perfect simple and the words below.

1. you / ever / teach / at a different school?

> Have you ever taught at a different school?

2. you / ever / teach / another subject?
3. you / ever / study / another language?
4. you / ever / have / a different kind of job?
5. you / ever / visit / _____?
6. you / ever / have / a student from / _____?

D Write two more questions to ask your teacher. Use the present perfect simple and *ever.*

1. Time expressions are usually placed at the end of a sentence.
   I have worked here **since 2005**. | I have worked here **for two years**.
   I have changed jobs **twice**. | She has taken four breaks **so far**!

2. Adverbs of frequency are often placed before the main verb in a sentence.
   Laura has **never** received a warning at work. | She has **always** been a great employee.

3. *Just* and *finally* are usually placed before the main verb in a sentence.
   Henry has **just** gotten a raise. | Andrea has **finally** finished her project.

4. *Already* is placed before the main verb or at the end of a sentence.
   They have **already** repaired three computers. | They have repaired three computers **already**.

5. *Yet* and *recently* are usually placed at the end of a sentence. *Yet* is usually used in questions and negative sentences.
   I've spoken to him **recently**. | Bill hasn't spoken to his supervisor **yet**.

A In groups, write three sentences about each picture: two sentences in the present perfect simple and one in the simple past. Use all the words in the boxes.

1. have a job interview

> just   twice   yesterday

3. take a vacation

> always   last summer   recently

2. get a promotion

> in 2015   twice   yet

4. complete the order

> already   an hour ago   finally

ACTIVE GRAMMAR — Contrast: Present Perfect Simple and Present Perfect Continuous

Some verbs can be used in either the present perfect simple or the present perfect continuous. When used in the present perfect simple, the verb shows the **result** of an action. When used in the present perfect continuous, the verb shows the **duration** or **continuation** of an action.

They **have worked** very hard on this project.

They **have been working** on this project since last month.

Other verbs, especially non-action verbs, can be used with the present perfect simple but not the present perfect continuous.

Jake **has needed** some help with his homework recently.

I **have owned** this car for ten years.

There are exceptions. Some verbs can show both action and non-action.

Maria **has been having** a good experience at this company.

More information in Appendix A.

A ACADEMIC Complete the sentences. Use the present perfect simple or the present perfect continuous. Either form can be used in some sentences. Then, discuss your answers. Which sentences focus on result and which focus on duration?

1. They (just / finish) _____ have just finished _____ cleaning the trucks.

2. I (live) _____ here for six months.

3. We (not / see) _____ the new schedules yet.

4. The manager (interview) _____ new job applicants this week.

5. My supervisor (ask) _____ for help with the new project five times already.

6. I (know) _____ her since we first came to this company.

7. That company (have) _____ a lot of problems lately.

8. I (work) _____ on this program all day.

9. Adam (not / wear) _____ jeans since the company policy changed.

10. They (already / complete) _____ four repairs.

11. Henry (not / leave) _____ early since the new supervisor started working here.

12. Alexandra (not / work) _____ overtime since she got a promotion.

13. Our supervisor (hire) _____ anyone new in over two months.

The simple past is often used to describe an action that happened at a specific time in the past. The action is complete.

I **finished** my deliveries an hour ago.

We **had to work** overtime from 5:00 to 8:00.

The present perfect simple is often used to describe an action that happened in the recent past, and is still true now. This action may continue in the future.

They**'ve** already **used** this equipment.

I**'ve applied** to that company twice, and I may apply again.

A ACADEMIC Complete the sentences. Use the simple past or the present perfect simple. Either form can be used in some sentences.

1. Bob (receive) _____ received _____ a raise last year.

2. Laura (have) _____ three interviews this week, but she (not / receive) _____ a job offer.

3. Samantha (have) _____ a job interview in Dallas yesterday.

4. We (already / hear) _____ that presentation many times.

5. I (never / see) _____ that presentation.

6. Sarah (take) _____ two sick days when she had the flu.

7. Ellen (take) _____ two sick days so far.

8. The company (already / hire) _____ three new employees, but we need one more.

9. My company (hire) _____ the four new employees that we needed.

B ACADEMIC **LET'S TALK.** Complete the questions. Then, ask and answer the questions with a partner. Use the simple present, simple past, present perfect simple, or present perfect continuous.

1. How long (you / study) _____ have you been studying _____ English?

2. When (you / start) _____ studying at this school?

3. (you / ever / study) _____ at another school?

4. Why (you / decide) _____ to study at this school?

5. How many different teachers (you / have) _____ at this school?

6. How many classes (you / take) _____ at this school?

C Listen. Circle the letter of the sentence with the correct meaning. 🎧 49

1. **a.** The doctor is still seeing patients.

   (b.) The doctor is finished seeing patients for the day.

2. **a.** Jamie is still ironing shirts.

   b. Jamie is finished ironing shirts for the day.

3. **a.** The men are still planting trees.

   b. The men are finished planting trees.

4. **a.** The teacher has more papers to correct.

   b. The teacher finished all the papers.

5. **a.** Carlos is finished for the day.

   b. Carlos is still in his truck, delivering packages.

6. **a.** Mary is not going to call any more people today.

   b. Mary will call 100 more people.

7. **a.** Jenna retired from the hospital.

   b. Jenna's still working at the hospital.

8. **a.** Tim will drive farther today.

   b. Tim's going to stop for the day.

D **Pronunciation: 've and 's** Listen and repeat. 🎧 50

1. **a.** I sold three cars.

   (b.) I've sold three cars.

2. **a.** She worked five hours.

   b. She's worked five hours.

3. **a.** They made 200 donuts.

   b. They've made 200 donuts.

4. **a.** She walked four miles.

   b. She's walked four miles.

5. **a.** I helped ten customers.

   b. I've helped ten customers.

6. **a.** He planted six trees.

   b. He's planted six trees.

7. **a.** She read 20 pages.

   b. She's read 20 pages.

8. **a.** I cleaned seven rooms.

   b. I've cleaned seven rooms.

E Listen again. Circle the sentence you hear in Exercise D. 🎧 51

F STUDENT TO STUDENT

Student 1: Turn to Appendix C. Read the **Set A** questions to Student 2.

Student 2: Listen to Student 1 and answer the questions about the pictures in complete sentences. Use the words in the boxes and the simple past or present perfect simple.

Then, change roles. Student 2 will read **Set B**, and Student 1 will write the answers under the pictures.

1.

fired one   hired three

4.

four doctors   ten patients

2.

eight years   five cars

5.

four years   one home

3.

at 5:00 a.m.   seven streets

6.

five years   two systems

THE BIG PICTURE | Job Performance

Bus driver Al Nywening retired after 42 years of working for the Toronto Transit Commission.

A **AT WORK** Listen and complete the job description. 🎧 52

Job Description for Metro Transit Drivers

1. All applicants must have an in-person _____interview_____, a _____background_____ check, and a _____drug_____ test.

2. Employee pay starts at $ _____ an hour.

3. Report to work on time and in _____.

4. Drive _____ and obey all _____ and safety laws.

5. _____ and drop off passengers at designated bus stops.

6. Greet and treat _____ politely.

7. All employees receive an _____ every year. If it's good, they receive a raise.

8. If an employee has no problems for four years, pay will increase to almost $ _____ an hour.

B **ACADEMIC** Listen again and answer the questions. 🎧 52

1. How long has George been working for Metro Transit? _____For eight years_____

2. What was George's job before this? _____

3. Why did he leave his first job? _____

4. What does George say to his passengers? _____

5. Does he know the names of his passengers? _____

6. Has he ever received an award? _____

C Listen. Then, listen again and write the questions to match the answers. Use the simple present, simple past, or present perfect simple. 🎧53

1. How much *overtime does George work* _____?

   About seven hours a week

2. How much _____?

   It's time and a half.

3. _____?

   Yes, he has gotten one.

4. Why _____?

   He received one because he went through a red light.

5. _____?

   No, he hasn't, but his friend got two.

6. _____?

   He likes it because the pay and the benefits are good.

D **ACADEMIC** Complete the sentences. Use the simple past or present perfect simple forms of the verbs.

1. Before he started at Metro Transit, George (work) _____ *worked* _____
   as a school bus driver.

2. He (not / like) _____ the noise on the school bus.

3. When George first began at Metro Transit, he (earn) _____
   $17 an hour.

4. He (receive) _____ many pay raises since then.

5. His performance evaluations (always / be) _____ very good.

6. He (only / have) _____ two or three passenger
   complaints, which is less than the company average.

7. Two years ago, he (get) _____ a ticket for going
   through a red light.

8. He (pay) _____ the fine, and the company (make)
   _____ him pay an additional fine.

9. George (always / be) _____ polite and courteous
   to the passengers.

A Discuss the questions.

1. What kinds of jobs do you think will be needed in the future?
2. Do you think your job or your family's jobs will be needed in the year 2040? Why?

WORD PARTNERSHIPS

service-providing	
goods-producing	jobs
health-related	

B Read the text. Then, match.

___c___ **1.** to age   **a.** to grow larger

_____ **2.** to increase   **b.** to cause to change in some way

_____ **3.** to be in demand   **c.** to get older

_____ **4.** to affect   **d.** to stay

_____ **5.** to remain   **e.** to be needed or wanted

READING NOTE

Finding Definitions

You can sometimes find the definition of a new or important word after a dash or a comma following the term.

Some baby boomers—people born between 1946 and 1964—are retiring.

C **ACADEMIC** Highlight or underline the definitions for the following terms in the text.

1. goods-producing jobs
2. service providers
3. *Occupational Outlook Handbook*

D **ACADEMIC** Circle *True* or *False*.

1. The workforce is getting younger.	True	(False)
2. Baby boomers are continuing to work because of vacation costs.	True	False
3. The jobs most in demand in the future will be service-providing jobs.	True	False
4. The government expects to see more jobs in medical fields.	True	False
5. A person who installs solar panels will have a good job outlook.	True	False
6. The government revises the *Occupational Outlook Handbook* every four years.	True	False

E **▶ WATCH** Watch the video and discuss the questions with a partner. Then, work in groups and write a job description for The Dogist. Include job requirements, skills, and responsibilities.

1. Do you think The Dogist has a goods-producing or service-providing job? Explain.
2. Do you think this job will be needed in 2040? Why?
3. Would you like to have this job? Why?

The Changing Workforce

The workforce of the United States includes everyone who is working now and everyone who is looking for a job. The Bureau of Labor Statistics evaluates the current workforce and employment opportunities. It makes predictions about the future.

There are approximately 155 million workers in the United States. What will the future workforce look like? One important change is that the workforce is **aging**. Many baby boomers—people born between 1946 and 1964—are **remaining** in their jobs longer than expected. In fact, the number of 64 to 75-year-olds in the workforce has risen more than any other age group. One reason for this may be that baby boomers want to add to their retirement benefits. Health costs have been **increasing**, and people have been living longer, so baby boomers want to work as long as they can. This has been a problem for younger workers because older workers have been staying in senior positions with higher salaries, preventing younger workers from getting promotions.

The kinds of jobs needed in the US have also been changing. The labor department divides jobs into two categories: goods-producing jobs and service-providing jobs. Goods-producing jobs—farming, manufacturing, mining—will show negative growth because most goods will be produced in other countries and many tasks will be done by machines. The government expects that most new job openings in the next ten years will be for service providers, or workers who give assistance to a customer or patient. Many of these jobs will require more than a high school degree. For example, physician assistants, physical therapist assistants, and other health care professionals will **be in demand** because of the rise of preventive care and the growing number of older people.

In addition, changes in energy and technology have been **affecting** jobs in the US. Solar panel installation and wind turbine service jobs are expected to grow more than 90 percent between 2016 and 2026. Also, there will be over 25 percent more software developers and computer and data security personnel needed in the near future.

Every two years, the US government publishes the *Occupational Outlook Handbook*, a document that presents specific information about the job market and job outlook. Some of the information included is salary, education required, and job responsibilities. This document can be found online or in the reference section of any local library and is useful for all job seekers. 🎧 54

Most solar photovoltaic installers need a high school diploma and receive up to a year of on-the-job training.

A Read.

Pamela Simmons

October 23

My Future Career

I have been considering a career as a dental hygienist. A dental hygienist usually works in a dentist's office. A dental hygienist removes plaque from teeth, takes dental X-rays, and tells patients how to clean and floss their teeth. In some offices, dental hygienists administer anesthetics, fill cavities, and assist the dentist.

All dental hygienists have to get a license from their state. It is necessary to attend an accredited dental hygiene program, so I've gone online to look for information about programs in my area. Students must pass a written and clinical examination. Many community colleges offer dental hygienist programs, and many dental hygienists who work in dental offices have an associate degree. Others have a bachelor's degree or even a doctorate.

Students in dental hygiene programs study in different settings. They study in classrooms, in laboratories, and in model dental offices. There is a strong job outlook for dental hygienists. In this field, people can work flexible hours or part time. The average salary is about $74,000 a year.

I'm interested in this career because I like working with people, and I like the medical field. Also, the working conditions are good. I don't have time to attend a four-year college, so a career that only requires a three-year program sounds good to me. I have been taking courses in biology, chemistry, and math to prepare for this path. Finally, I've always cared about my teeth, so I think this will be a great career for me.

B **CIVICS** Check your job skills. Then, discuss your skills with a partner.

- ☐ sales
- ☐ managing money
- ☐ writing
- ☐ organizing
- ☐ operating equipment

- ☐ drawing
- ☐ designing
- ☐ working with numbers
- ☐ working with people
- ☐ designing websites

- ☐ doing physical work
- ☐ repairing equipment
- ☐ teaching
- ☐ public speaking
- ☐ helping people

C **AT WORK** Discuss the meaning of each job characteristic. Then, check the characteristics that are the most important to you.

☐ salary   ☐ benefits   ☐ job training

☐ job status   ☐ job security   ☐ flexibility

☐ opportunities for promotion   ☐ opportunities for travel

D **CIVICS** Go online. Use the *Occupational Outlook Handbook* to research a job that interests you. Complete the chart below or record the information in your notebook.

Career title	
Job description	
Working conditions	
Education or training	
Earnings	
Job outlook	

WRITING NOTE

Citing Online Sources

When using research in a paper, you must **cite**, or list, your sources. Your sources should go in a list at the end of your paper called the **works cited** page. One method for citing sources comes from the MLA (Modern Language Association). Below is a citation of a website in MLA format. Pay attention to the punctuation.

"Registered Nurses." *Occupational Outlook Handbook*, U.S. Bureau of Labor Statistics, 13 Apr. 2018, www.bls.gov/ooh/healthcare/registered-nurses.html.

"Article Title." *Website Title*, Website Publisher, date of article, web address.

E **ACADEMIC** Write a few paragraphs about the job you chose to research. Explain why this career is a good choice for you. Include a works cited page in MLA format at the end of your paper.

F Find and correct the mistakes.

1. I have never ~~take~~ *taken* a sick day.
2. She has gotten along with her coworkers always.
3. She has receive an award for the top salesperson twice.
4. Have you never had a performance review?
5. She has been writing two reports so far.

A **AT WORK** Katie is a sales assistant. Read her job description.

Davis Jewelry: Sales Assistant
Assist customers.
Maintain and restock displays.
Enter sales information accurately.
Follow all store procedures and polices.

B **AT WORK** Listen to Katie's performance evaluation. Check the correct boxes. 🎧55

	Meets / Exceeds Expectations	Shows Improvement	Needs Improvement	Unsatisfactory
Appearance is professional	✔			
Arrives at work on time				
Shows initiative				
Assists customers effectively				
Enters sales information accurately				
Works well under pressure				

C **LET'S TALK.** With a partner, discuss Katie's work performance.

1. Has Katie always arrived on time? Has her on-time arrival improved?

2. How is Katie's customer service? How are her sales techniques?

3. When does Katie make mistakes?

4. What has Mr. Davis decided to do?

REGRETS AND POSSIBILITIES

AT WORK Identify possible explanations for workplace situations

ACADEMIC Infer information from an image; scan a text for key words and identify the meanings from context; use quotation marks and punctuation correctly; understand and apply note-taking methods

CIVICS Express opinions about language and cultural programs

A skydiving instructor (back) and passenger (front) jump out of an airplane.

1.

"I should have studied English before I came to this country."

2.

"I shouldn't have stayed out so late last night."

3.

"I should have learned how to drive."

4.

"I shouldn't have turned down that other job."

5.

"I should have paid attention in math class."

6.

"I shouldn't have taken an evening class."

7.

"I should have moved to a warmer city."

8.

"I shouldn't have eaten all that junk food."

ACTIVE GRAMMAR | *Should have* for Regrets

I You We They He She	should have should not have shouldn't have	taken the bus. opened the box.

Should have / Shouldn't have can be used to express regret about a past action.

I **should have studied** more.
(Meaning: I didn't study enough.)

They **shouldn't have left** their umbrellas at home.
(Meaning: It rained; they weren't prepared.)

More information in Appendix A.

A Write the past participle form of each verb.

1. buy _____bought_____
2. fill _____
3. break _____

4. feel _____
5. meet _____
6. see _____

7. sleep _____
8. try _____
9. eat _____

B Pronunciation: *should have / shouldn't have* Listen and repeat. 🎧56

1. **a.** We should have left at 3 o'clock.
   b. We shouldn't have left at 3 o'clock.
2. **a.** They should have been there.
   b. They shouldn't have been there.
3. **a.** She should have brought her backpack.
   b. She shouldn't have brought her backpack.
4. **a.** I should have taken a nap.
   b. I shouldn't have taken a nap.

C Listen and circle the letter of the sentence you hear. Then, practice the sentences with a partner. 🎧57

D Listen and complete with *should have* or *shouldn't have* and the past participle you hear. 🎧58

1. I _____should have bought_____ a new one.
2. She _____ harder.
3. I _____ so many courses.
4. I _____ earlier.
5. I _____ to bring it.
6. They _____ the tank.
7. He _____ without one.
8. She _____ it.

E Complete the sentences. Use *should have* or *shouldn't have* and the past participle of the verbs in parentheses.

1. I registered for too many courses, and now my grades are falling.

   I (take) _____ *shouldn't have taken* _____ so many courses.

2. Akiko forgot to bring her book, and she needs it for the exam.

   She (forget) _____ her book.

3. Sandra's cellphone rang during the exam.

   She (turn off) _____ her phone before the exam.

4. Jim stayed up very late. The next morning, he overslept and was late.

   He (stay up) _____ so late.

5. Marie wanted to take a psychology course, but she registered too late.

   She (register) _____ earlier.

6. Paul didn't edit his paper, so he received a low grade.

   He (edit) _____ his paper.

F **ACADEMIC** **LET'S TALK.** With a partner, make a statement about each picture. Use words from the box, *should have* or *shouldn't have*, and your imagination.

bring	eat	put	remember	take	wear

1.

2.

3.

4.

5.

6.

ACTIVE GRAMMAR | *Should have* for Expectations

Should have / Shouldn't have can be used to describe expectations about the past that were not met.

The bus **should have arrived** by now.
(Meaning: The bus is late.)

I **shouldn't have gotten** a D on this exam.
(Meaning: My grade is lower than expected.)

A **ACADEMIC** Listen and write the number under the correct picture. 🎧 59

a. _____

c. _____

e. _____1_____

b. _____

d. _____

f. _____

B Complete the sentences. Use *should have* or *shouldn't have* and the past participle of the verbs in parentheses.

1. Our professor isn't here. She (arrive) ___*should have arrived*___ at 9:00.

2. Why hasn't the movie started? It (begin) _____ at 8:20.

3. Paul hasn't gotten his degree yet, but he (graduate) _____ last semester.

4. The library (not / charge) _____ me a late fee. There was a snowstorm yesterday.

5. The contractors (not / replace) _____ the carpet. It was brand-new!

6. It's 4:00. Lina (find) _____ out if she was accepted into the new math program.

7. The snow (stop) _____, according to the weather forecast.

Regrets and Possibilities **149**

ACTIVE GRAMMAR | *May have, Might have, Could have* for Past Possibilities

> *May (not) have*, *might (not) have*, and *could have* can be used to express past possibilities.
>   They **may have gone** to the movies.
>   He **might not have remembered** to bring the tickets.
>   She **could have bought** a new car.
> *Could not have* (*couldn't have*) can be used to express past impossibilities.
>   You **couldn't have been** at work that day. You were in the emergency room with your daughter.

More information in Appendix A.

A **AT WORK** Match each statement with the correct possibility.

_____e__ **1.** Frank didn't come to work yesterday.

_____ **2.** I wonder where James went. He was gone for 15 minutes.

_____ **3.** I think I heard an ambulance siren. What happened?

_____ **4.** Marco was wearing a suit yesterday. He usually wears jeans.

_____ **5.** Angie looks a little sad. I wonder what happened.

_____ **6.** Anna talked to the supervisor yesterday.

_____ **7.** I can't find my cellphone.

a. He could have had a job interview.

b. He may have taken a break.

c. She might not have gotten that promotion.

d. You couldn't have left it at home. I saw you with it a minute ago.

e. He may have been sick.

f. She could have told him about her problem with her coworker.

g. There might have been an accident.

B Read each sentence. With a partner, write two possibilities in your notebooks. Use *might (not) have*, *may (not) have*, or *could have* and a verb.

1. There were a lot of cars parked in front of your neighbor's house.

2. Your friend didn't want to come to the movies with you yesterday.

3. You were surprised that your brother didn't answer your phone call.

4. A classmate missed an important exam.

5. Your professor canceled class today.

6. Your friend got a bad sunburn.

What do you think happened?

ACTIVE GRAMMAR | *Must have* for Inferences

Must (not) have can be used to express an inference about a past action. An inference is a guess about something that seems true.

Situation: I don't have my keys with me. I left the house this morning, and I think the keys were on the kitchen table. I don't remember locking the door.

Inferences: I **must have left** my keys at home.

I **must not have remembered** to bring my keys.

More information in Appendix A.

CULTURE NOTE

Call 911 to report an emergency to the police, fire department, or emergency medical services.

A **ACADEMIC** Listen. A man is calling 911 to report a problem in his apartment. Write the letter of the correct inference under each picture. 🎧 60

1. _____ *g*

3. _____

5. _____

7. _____

2. _____

4. _____

6. _____

8. _____

a. The burglar must have used the suitcase to steal the shirts.

b. The burglar must have taken it.

c. The burglar must have dropped the gloves when he left.

d. The burglar must have scared the cat.

e. The burglar must have left through the window.

f. The burglar must have been hungry.

g. Someone must have broken in.

h. The burglar must have put on your suit.

B **Pronunciation:** *must have / might have / could have* Listen and repeat. Then, practice saying the sentences with a partner. 🎧 61

1. You must have left your book at home.
2. She might have studied French.
3. He might have missed the appointment.
4. We could have gone on a vacation.

5. He must have been at work.
6. She couldn't have walked that far.
7. You must have told her.
8. They could have taken the bus.

C **Pronunciation: Sentence Stress** Listen to the conversation and underline the stressed words. 🎧 62

A: <u>Hi</u>, <u>Julia</u>. <u>Why</u> didn't you <u>come</u> to my <u>party</u>? Everyone <u>missed</u> you.

B: What party?

A: I had a Fourth of July party last Saturday.

B: Really? You should have called me.

A: I did. I left a message on your voicemail.

B: I changed my number. You could have sent me an invitation.

A: I did. I emailed it two weeks ago.

B: You must have sent it to the wrong address. I got a new account.

A: You should have told me.

B: Sorry! Anyway, how was the party?

A: It was fun. You should have been there!

> **Sentence Stress**
> Stress the content words in a sentence. Content words give meaning to the sentence. Question words, main verbs, adjectives, and nouns are usually stressed.
> You should have **called** me.

D Practice the conversation in Exercise C with a partner. Use the correct stress.

The Fourth of July is US Independence Day. Many Americans celebrate with barbecues, sparklers, and fireworks.

ACTIVE GRAMMAR | *Must have* for Empathy

> *Must have* can be used to express empathy about the past. When used with adjectives, the form is usually *must have* + past participle of *be* + adjective.
>
> **A:** My daughter didn't make the soccer team.
> **B:** She **must have been** disappointed.

A **LET'S TALK.** With a partner, take turns reading and responding to the statements. Use the subjects in parentheses, *must have been*, and the adjectives from the box.

| angry | ~~bored~~ | disgusted | embarrassed | excited | proud |

> We spent ten very long hours at the museum.

> You must have been bored.

1. We spent ten very long hours at the museum. (You)
2. We saw one of our favorite singers in a cafe. (You)
3. They ordered soup, and there was a cockroach in one of the bowls. (They)
4. I was talking about my boss when she walked into the room. (You)
5. We were taking a test when my cellphone rang. (Your teacher)
6. My sister was the first person in our family to graduate from college. (Your family)

B **STUDENT TO STUDENT**

Student 1: Turn to Appendix C and follow the instructions. Then, switch roles and read sentences 6-10.

Student 2: Read sentences 1-5 about last weekend to Student 1. Then, switch roles. Turn to Appendix C and follow the instructions.

> My homework was very difficult.

> You must have been frustrated.

1. I had to work overtime all weekend.
2. I couldn't find my keys for two hours.
3. I didn't get the job.
4. My son's team won the championship!
5. My brother got a promotion.
6. My daughter got engaged.
7. I got lost for an hour in a bad neighborhood because a road was blocked.
8. I had a problem at the bank, and I couldn't express myself in English.
9. I received a bonus at work.
10. My friends had a birthday party for me.

A **ACADEMIC** A high school counselor is talking to Amber, a student. Listen and take notes below. 🎧63

Notes about Amber	Notes about Miguel

B **ACADEMIC** The counselor is talking to Miguel, another student. Listen and take notes above. 🎧64

C Write the correct letter to match the students with their problems.

Amber ____*a*____   **a.** problems with the soccer team

        _____   **b.** problems with a class

        _____   **c.** college plans

Miguel _____   **d.** poor grades

        _____   **e.** needed a job

        _____   **f.** lost a job

D Listen again to Amber's conversation. Then, answer the questions. 🎧 **63**

1. What job did Amber have at school?
2. What does the counselor think about Amber's work on the school newspaper?
3. Why is Amber upset?
4. Was Amber good at her job?
5. Why is the job important to her?
6. What did Amber do wrong? Why did she do it?
7. Is she sorry?
8. What is the counselor going to do to help her?

E Complete the sentences. Use *should have* or *shouldn't have* and the past participle of the verb in parentheses to express your opinions.

1. Amber (write) _____ false information.

2. Amber (speak) _____ to the soccer coach about her feelings.

3. Amber (think) _____ more carefully before she wrote the article.

4. In my opinion, the vice principal (take) _____ away her job.

F Listen to Miguel's conversation again. Then, answer the questions. 🎧 **64**

1. Has Miguel's schoolwork improved?
2. Did Miguel do the things that the counselor suggested?
3. How did Miguel improve his math grade?
4. Which is harder for Miguel—speaking English or writing English?
5. Why didn't Miguel go back to the writing center?
6. Where is Miguel working now?
7. What is Miguel's work schedule?

G Complete the sentences. Use *must have, could have,* or *couldn't have* and the past participle of the verb in parentheses.

1. Miguel (find) _____*could have found*_____ a math tutor, but he didn't need to.

2. Miguel's math instructor (be) _____ pleased with his progress.

3. Miguel (make) _____ a good impression at his job interview.

4. Miguel (find) _____ a different writing tutor.

5. Miguel (get) _____ the job without his counselor's help.

A Read the personal stories.

Family 1

"I'm from Argentina. My family and I have been living in the United States for almost three years now. My children can speak English fluently, but they don't speak Spanish anymore. I'm afraid that they may have forgotten our language. My wife and I could have spoken Spanish with them at home, but we wanted them to practice English. We should have helped them maintain our language and learn about our culture, but it's too late now."

Family 2

"My daughter is very excited. This summer, we're going to visit my parents in Japan. I've been sending her to a Japanese school every weekend for the past year. Friends told me that I should have focused on her English, but my husband and I wanted her to learn Japanese, too. She's been writing letters to her grandparents, and they are thrilled to receive messages that they can read. We must have made the right decision."

READING NOTE

Preparing to Read

Before you read an article, read the title. Then, read the first two sentences of each paragraph. What do you already know about the topic? Finally, read the article from the beginning.

B **CIVICS** Discuss the questions. Then, read the text on the following page.

1. Can the children in your family speak, read, and write your native language?

2. Do you want the children to learn your native language and learn about your culture? Why?

C **ACADEMIC** Find the boldfaced words in the reading. Circle the correct definition for each word.

1. **Maintain** means . . .
   a. to write.   **b.** to be disappointed.   **c.** to continue having.   **d.** to speak.

2. A **mission** is . . .
   a. a goal.   **b.** a map.   **c.** a lesson.   **d.** a fight.

3. Which of the following is a **fine art**?
   a. drawing   **b.** math   **c.** chemistry   **d.** biology

4. *It was a **struggle*** means . . .
   a. it was boring.   **b.** it was confusing.   **c.** it was difficult.   **d.** it was exciting.

Language and Cultural Programs

What can immigrant parents do to help their children learn about or **maintain** their native language and culture? Children who grow up speaking one language outside the home and a different language inside the home learn to speak two languages. However, it is often hard for these children to read and write their parents' native language at an advanced level. Therefore, many parents send their children to special programs for at least a few hours a week. The **mission** of these programs is to help children with immigrant parents and/or grandparents to learn the native language and culture. There are Polish, Chinese, and Russian schools, to name a few.

One Korean school in New York City offers instruction every Saturday. The school teaches reading and conversation, Korean history, and Korean **fine arts**, including art and music. Students include Korean, American, and Korean-American children.

A Greek Orthodox Church in Chicago runs a school that teaches children to read, write, and speak Greek. Classes are about three hours every Saturday. One parent explained why she sent her child to the Greek school. She said, "I studied Greek in an after-school program when I was a child, and I wanted my daughter to learn it, too. While learning the culture of my parents, she also learned another language. The more languages she learns, the better off she'll be in the future." She added, "Sometimes it was a **struggle** to get her to classes, in terms of convenience and other school activities, but I kept her in them." When the girl was older, she even took a trip to Greece with her classmates from the school. 🎧65

Seven-year-old Cara Lee learns Chinese calligraphy with her mother's help.

D **CIVICS** Discuss the questions.

1. What do you think about language and cultural programs? Do you know someone who should have gone to a program like these?

2. Do you think it's important for children to learn to speak, read, and write their parents' or grandparents' native language? Why?

A Read.

Manny Arias
March 21

My Regrets

    It's difficult to move to a new city, especially in a new country. Looking back, there are many things that I should have done to prepare for the move from my country to the United States.

    First of all, the new language made things difficult. I studied English in high school, but I didn't take it seriously. I should have studied harder. Also, I could have taken English classes before I came here. Of course, I'm studying English now, but it might have been easier if I had taken classes before.

    Second, good jobs are hard to find. I finished my degree back in my country, but when I spoke with a college admissions counselor in the US, she asked, "Do you have copies of your transcripts?" Now, it's difficult to get the transcripts; I should have brought them with me. I've ordered my transcripts from the university, but it's taking a long time for them to arrive. When they arrive, I may be able to find a job in my field or use some of my credits toward a new degree in the US.

    Finally, I didn't know how to drive when I arrived. In my country, public transportation was very convenient and cheap. But in this state, many jobs are outside of the city, and there isn't any public transportation to those locations. One of my friends is teaching me how to drive, but I should have learned earlier. Those are a few of the things that I could have done before I came here.

B You are going to write about your regrets or things you wish that you could have changed or done differently when you moved to this country. Answer the questions to give you some ideas.

1. What did you forget to bring with you to this country that you needed?
2. What did you bring with you that you didn't need?
3. What should you have done before you came here?
4. Could you have studied English before you came to this country?
5. Where did you live when you first came to this country?
6. Did you have information about job opportunities before you came to this country? Were you happy with your first job?

WRITING NOTE

Quotation Marks

Use quotation marks to write someone's exact words. Report exact words with verbs such as *said, shouted, yelled, cried, asked,* or *complained.* Notice that there is a comma after *said* in the sentence below. Also, the period at the end of the sentence is inside the quotation marks.

> She said**,** **"**I studied Greek in an after-school program when I was a child, and I wanted my daughter to learn Greek, too**."**

C **ACADEMIC** Complete the sentences. Use the verbs from the box. Add punctuation.

asked	complained	explained	said	shouted

1. Sylvia _____ *shouted,* _____ "Stop slamming the door!"

2. Ivan _____ When can I take the test

3. Marlene _____ We should have called the police

4. Juliette _____ Do you have any job openings

5. Karen _____ I overslept. I'm sorry I'm late

6. Al _____ I've lived here a long time, and you've never visited me

7. José _____ You should have invited her to the party

D Write a few paragraphs using your ideas from Exercise B. Use quotation marks at least once.

E **ACADEMIC** Read your partner's text. Underline the punctuation around quotations. Did your partner use it correctly? What does your partner regret?

F Find and correct the mistakes.

1. I could have ~~study~~ *studied* to be a doctor, but I chose to study computers instead.

2. We should have not eaten so much. I think I've gained five pounds!

3. You must had enjoyed the party.

4. Peter might has called after 10:00.

5. Edward should enjoyed his surprise party, but he didn't.

6. That TV must have be expensive. It's the newest model.

7. The performance last night must be exciting.

8. She might been upset when I called.

Regrets and Possibilities **159**

A `ACADEMIC` Read.

It is difficult to take good notes on a lecture. The following tips may help.

1. Before the lecture, think about the topic. What do you already know about it?

2. Listen for cues that will help you understand the lecture. For example:

   a. *First*, *second*, *third*, … These words can introduce steps in a process.

   b. *In addition, moreover*, and *furthermore* … These words introduce more information.

3. Use the following note-taking method to both organize your notes and study after class. Draw lines on your paper like the example below.

   a. Take notes on the right side of the page.

   - Write key words, phrases, or short sentences.
   - Use titles, bullet points, and numbering to organize your notes.
   - Copy any definitions exactly as you hear them.

   b. After taking notes, write example test questions about the information on the left side of the page.

   - After the lecture, write or say the answers to your questions.

   c. Think about the important ideas in the lecture and write a summary of your notes at the bottom of the page.

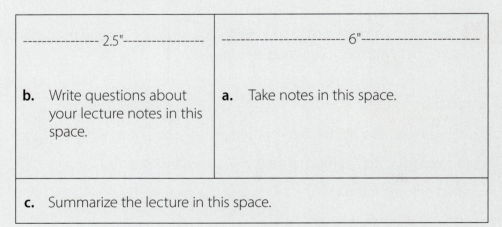

4. Quiz yourself using the questions you wrote a few times a week for ten minutes or more.

B `ACADEMIC` Go online. Search for free lectures for ESL students. Listen to one of the lectures, and take notes using the method above.

BUSINESS AND INDUSTRY

Crab fishermen surrounded by their catch on a fishing boat off the coast of Alaska.

AT WORK Identify and recall information about the production processes

ACADEMIC Recall key details from a text; differentiate between the pros and cons of an issue; illustrate a statement with examples; present research findings in a group

CIVICS Identify industries in the US and around the world; read and create maps; discuss alternative energy sources

CIVICS Look at the map of the western United States. Answer the questions.

1. Which state is located north of California?

2. Which state is located west of Nevada?

3. Which country is located north of Idaho?

4. Which states are located south of Montana?

5. How many states are bordered by Colorado? Name the states.

6. How many states are bordered by Arizona? Name the states.

7. Which states are located to the north of Texas?

8. Which country is located to the southwest of Texas?

Subject	*Be*		Past Participle	
Cotton	is	grown		in Texas.
	is not			in Washington.
Computer chips	are	manufactured		in New Mexico.
	are not			in Oklahoma.

Active sentences usually emphasize the person or thing that does the action.
    Fishermen **catch** salmon in Washington.
Passive sentences usually emphasize the person or thing that receives the action.
    Salmon **are caught** in Washington.

More information in Appendix A.

A Write each product from the box under the correct verb in the chart. Use a dictionary to help you.

Count Nouns			Non-count Nouns	
~~apples~~	grapes	sheep (plural)	~~coal~~	lettuce
~~cattle (plural)~~	~~lumber products~~	~~shrimp~~ (plural)	copper	milk
chili peppers	pears	tomatoes	cotton	natural gas
computer chips	potatoes	tuna (plural)	gold	petroleum
~~computers~~	salmon (plural)		hay	wheat

mine	catch	grow
coal,	shrimp,	apples,

manufacture	produce	raise
computers,	lumber products,	cattle,

B In your notebook, write ten sentences about the map on the previous page, five with count nouns and five with non-count nouns. Two sentences must be negative. Use the simple present passive.

Tomatoes are grown in California.

C Circle the correct forms of the verbs.

1. Farmers **(grow)** / **are grown** corn in Indiana.

2. Hogs **raise** / **(are raised)** in Illinois.

3. Milk **produces** / **is produced** in Wisconsin.

4. Auto companies **manufacture** / **are manufactured** cars in Michigan.

5. Cars **don't manufacture** / **aren't manufactured** in Virginia.

6. Steel **produces** / **is produced** in Indiana.

7. Coal **mines** / **is mined** in Illinois.

8. Many companies **produce** / **is produced** cereal in Michigan.

9. Farmers **don't grow** / **are not grown** tomatoes in Wisconsin.

10. Cattle **raise** / **are raised** in Tennessee.

D **CIVICS** **LET'S TALK.** Work with a partner. Ask and answer *Yes / No* questions about the map.

Is milk produced in Wisconsin?

Yes, it is.

Are horses raised in Michigan?

No, they aren't.

WORD PARTNERSHIPS	
grow	vegetables
	flowers
	trees
raise	animals
	children

| Where | **is** | rice | **grown**? | Rice **is grown** in many Asian countries. |
| How | **are** | cars | **manufactured**? | Cars **are manufactured** on assembly lines in factories. |

A   **CIVICS**   Listen and write the questions you hear. Then, look at the map and write the answers in your notebook in complete sentences. 🎧66

Plural Count Nouns			Non-count Nouns			
cars	electronics	soybeans	clothing	copper	footwear	rice
cellphones	financial services	textiles	coal	corn	iron	wheat

1. <u>Where are electronics manufactured?</u>

2. _____

3. _____

4. _____

5. _____

6. _____

B   **LET'S TALK.** In your notebook, write three more *Wh-* questions about the map. Ask and answer the questions with a partner.

In passive sentences, include the person or thing that does the action when it is important and not obvious. Use *by*.

This candy is produced **by Royal Sweets**.

This toy is made **by an American company**.

More information in Appendix A.

A Rewrite the sentences in the simple present passive. Use *by* when necessary.

1. Farmers grow rice in Louisiana.

   Rice is grown in Louisiana.

2. A technician usually does my blood tests.

   My blood tests are usually done by a technician.

3. Cardiologists perform heart surgery.

   _____

4. Construction workers build skyscrapers in New York City.

   _____

5. In Maine, fishermen trap lobsters.

   _____

6. All over the world, people watch the World Cup.

   _____

7. Bob's Landscaping Co. cuts my neighbor's lawn.

   _____

8. Specially-trained bakers design wedding cakes.

   _____

9. My favorite autobody shop checks my car's fluids and tires.

   _____

10. Farmers grow cranberries in New Jersey and Massachusetts.

    _____

B **LET'S TALK.** Work in a group of three or four students. Take turns talking about the products in the photos. Use the simple present passive and the words in the box.

| deliver | design | make | manufacture | produce | sell |

> Gasoline is produced by many oil companies, such as
> _____. It is used by cars, trucks, and other vehicles
> _{company name(s)}
> and machines. I usually buy _____ gasoline.
> _{company name}

1.

5.

9.

2.

6.

10.

3.

7.

11.

4.

8.

12.

C Look around your home. Choose four products that you use. Answer the questions in your notebook.

1. What product do you or your family use?
2. Which company is it made / manufactured / designed by?
3. What is it used for?

My family and I use paper towels. They are made by Clean Green. They are used to wipe up spills

and clean the house.

Pronunciation: Stress in Word Forms Listen and repeat. 🎧 67

Verb	Adjective	Noun
1. pasteurize	pasteurized	pasteurization
2. sterilize	sterilized	sterilization
3. immunize	immunized	immunization
4. separate	separated	separation
5. refrigerate	refrigerated	refrigeration
6. evaporate	evaporated	evaporation
7. ferment	fermented	fermentation

> Many nouns end with *-tion*. The stressed syllable in these words usually comes before the *-tion* ending.
> action   education   emotion

E   Listen again. Underline the stressed syllable of each word in the chart above. 🎧 67

F   With a partner, find the above words in the dictionary and check the stress. Then, read the definitions of the words. For each row of words, choose one word to write in a sentence.

Most people in the US buy pasteurized milk.

G   **AT WORK** Match each set of words below to the correct picture on the following page. Use the words to write a sentence describing the process of gathering cacao beans. Two sentences require active verbs, and the others use passive verbs.

> the beans / export / to chocolate makers all over the world
> ~~the ripe pods / gather / every few weeks during the season~~
> the seeds / dry / by machine or by the sun
> the seed pulp / drain / for six to eight days
> the workers / cut down / the pods / from the cacao trees
> the seeds / put / in large wooden boxes / for fermentation
> the pods / split open / and the seeds / remove
> the workers / put / the seeds / into large sacks

Cacao beans are grown in many countries, including Ecuador, Ghana, and Indonesia.

1.

The ripe pods are gathered every few weeks during the season.

2.

_____

_____

3.

_____

_____

4.

_____

_____

5.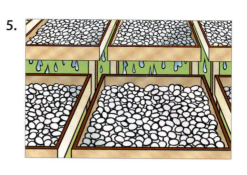

_____

_____

6.

_____

_____

7.

_____

_____

8.

_____

_____

A **AT WORK** Look at the pictures and describe the process in groups. Then, listen and take notes. 🎧 68

1.

2.

3.
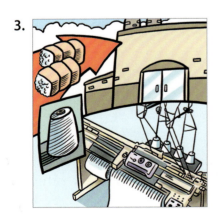

4.
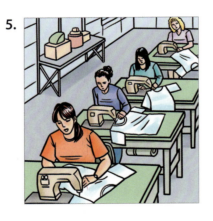

5.

6.

7.

8.

9.
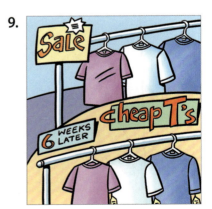

B **AT WORK** Listen again and answer the questions. 🎧68

1. Which countries are the top three cotton producers in the world?
   China, the United States, and India
2. What are the two ways that cotton can be picked?
3. Where is the cotton cleaned?
4. What happens at the cotton or textile mill?
5. What part of the production process uses a large amount of water?
6. Does one person sew an entire T-shirt? Explain.
7. What is the original cost of a T-shirt?
8. Why is the T-shirt price increased in the warehouse?
9. How much are the T-shirts sold for at the department store?
10. How long does it take before the T-shirts are sent to discount stores?

C Complete the sentences. Use the active or passive forms of the verbs in the box.

clean	dye	embroider	knit	~~pick~~	sell	send	sew	ship

1. Some cotton _____ *is picked* _____ by workers.
2. The cotton _____ at the ginner.
3. The bales of cotton _____ to cotton mills.
4. Knitting machines _____ the cotton yarn into fabric.
5. The dye houses _____ the fabric different colors.
6. The fabric _____ to a sewing plant.
7. The T-shirts _____ together piece by piece.
8. The printers _____ designs on the T-shirts.

D Complete the sentences. Use an active or passive verb.

1. After the patterns are cut, the workers _____ *sew the pieces* _____.
2. When the T-shirts are sold to the department stores, the price
   _____ by around 200 percent.
3. The prices _____ because the stores
   _____ for salespeople and other costs.
4. Before a T-shirt is discounted, the store _____ it at full price.
5. The leftover T-shirts _____ to discount
   stores, where _____ $9 or less.

A wind farm in Alberta, Canada.

A RENEWABLE ENERGY SOURCE

Hybrid and electric cars are becoming more and more popular. Hybrid cars use both gasoline and batteries to supply power to an electric motor. Electric cars use only electricity to power the engine. Because these cars are gaining in popularity, charging stations, places where drivers can recharge their hybrid and electric cars, are appearing in more cities. Consumers need clean energy to run these cars and to power electronics such as TVs, computers, and cellphones. What new power sources are being used to help protect our environment?

A significant source of **green**, or environmentally safe, energy is wind. For hundreds of years, windmills have been used by farmers to pump water. Today, millions of windmills and wind turbine engines are found throughout the world. Cities such as Rock Port, Missouri and Aspen, Colorado have been using significant amounts of wind energy to generate power for their communities. About 39 percent of California's power is generated by wind turbines. The top wind energy producers in the world are China, the United States, and Germany.

Wind has advantages over other energy sources, such as coal and gas. Wind energy does not generate harmful emissions, like carbon dioxide, so it is healthier for humans and the environment. It is also an energy source that doesn't run out, no matter how much energy households **consume**, or use. In addition, wind energy can create income for people who own groups of wind turbines, or **wind farms**, and smaller turbines can generate power for individual homes or businesses.

Although wind is a clean source of energy, not everyone is in favor of wind turbines. First, some **opponents** of wind energy say that large birds may fly into the moving parts and be killed. Some **advocates**, or supporters, of wind energy say that more birds are killed by cars than by wind turbines. Second, some opponents say that wind turbines are noisy and disturb neighborhoods. Some advocates say that wind turbines are no louder than refrigerators. Third, some residents complain that wind turbines are ugly and reduce the value of their properties. However, one wind advocacy group says that 99% of the turbines are in rural areas and that the turbines can generate tourism and well-paying jobs. In fact, wind turbine technicians can expect a strong job outlook. There are both pros and cons of wind energy, but it looks as though it is here to stay. 🎧 69

A **CIVICS** Discuss the questions. Then, read the text.

1. Can you name two sources of renewable energy?
2. How can today's cars be more environmentally friendly?

READING NOTE

Listing Pros and Cons

Some texts discuss the pros and cons of an issue. Pros are reasons why something may be good, and cons are reasons why something may be bad. As you read, make a list of the pros and cons that are discussed. This will help you understand the text more easily.

B **ACADEMIC** Answer the questions.

1. What were windmills originally used for?
2. Which cities are using wind as a significant source of clean energy?
3. How much of California's power comes from wind turbines?
4. What are the advantages of wind energy over coal and gas?
5. Can wind turbines generate power for individual homes?
6. Which countries are the top three producers of wind energy in the world?

C **ACADEMIC** Complete the definitions.

1. A **hybrid** car uses both _____ gasoline and batteries _____ to power an electric motor.
2. **Green** energy is _____ energy.
3. Households **consume**, or _____, a lot of energy.
4. A **wind farm** is _____ wind turbines.
5. **Opponents** of wind energy are people who _____ wind energy.
6. **Advocates** of wind energy are _____ of this energy choice.

D **ACADEMIC** Read the sentences. Write *Pro* or *Con*.

1. Windmills send no pollutants into the air.   _____ Pro _____
2. Wind energy may harm birds.   _____
3. Wind turbine generators can be noisy.   _____
4. Wind turbines may lower property value.   _____
5. Wind turbines can generate tourism.   _____
6. Wind turbines can create well-paying jobs.   _____

A Read.

Tokyo, Japan.

Hideo Tokuda
April 20

Business and Industry in Japan

I am from Tokyo, Japan. Tokyo is located in the eastern part of Japan on Honshu, the largest of the four main islands of Japan. Tokyo is also the capital city. Japan has a very large population. It is bordered by the Pacific Ocean to the east, the Sea of Japan to the west, and the East China Sea to the southwest. Many natural resources, such as wood and natural gas, are not found in my country, so they must be imported.

Rice is an important product for Japanese people. Rice is grown in many parts of Japan. Many vegetables, including sugar beets and radishes, and fruit, such as strawberries and grapes, are grown in Japan. Fishing used to be a large industry in Japan, but it has declined a lot in recent years.

Japan is best known for its cars and electronics. Three of the largest automobile companies in the world are Japanese. Japan is also known for its consumer electronics. For example, many televisions and game consoles are manufactured by Japanese companies. Look around your home. How many Japanese-made electronic devices can you find?

WRITING NOTE

Introducing Examples

For example, *such as*, and *including* all introduce examples, but they are used in different ways. Note the punctuation and placement of the examples.

Many minerals, **such as** copper and iron ore, can be found in my country.

Many industries are in trouble right now. **For example**, two steel plants have laid off workers.

Tourists can visit a number of famous places in Japan, **including** Kyoto and Mt. Fuji.

B **ACADEMIC** Complete the sentences with examples.

1. Dye houses dye T-shirts a variety of colors, such as _____

   and _____.

2. T-shirts are sold at discounted prices at many stores, including

   _____, _____, and _____.

3. There are many countries represented in my class. For example, there are students from

   _____, _____, and _____.

4. My country has natural resources _____

   _____.

5. Agricultural products _____ are grown in my country.

C **CIVICS** In your notebook, draw a map of your native country. Show the bordering countries. Then, add products and natural resources. Go online to find any information you don't know.

D **CIVICS** Write about your native country's industries and products. Use the questions to guide you.

1. What city and country are you from? Where is it located?
2. What are three major products that are produced in your country?
3. What are some of the major industries or businesses in your country?
4. What natural resources are found in your country?

E **ACADEMIC** Read your partner's text and answer the questions.

1. What city and country is your partner from?
2. What are three products that are produced in your partner's country?
3. What natural resources does your partner's country have?

F Find and correct the mistakes.

1. Coffee is ~~grow~~ *grown* in South and Central America.
2. Italy is bordering by Switzerland, France, Austria, and Slovenia.
3. After the cotton picked, it is sent to the ginner.
4. France and Italy is known for their fashion industries.
5. Dairy cows are grown by Swiss farmers.
6. The buildings are owned ACE Property Management.

A **LET'S TALK.** Work in groups of three or four students. Choose a state to research.

B **CIVICS** Go online. Find information about the state you chose. Draw a map of the state in the space below. Mark important places and products on your map.

1. Put a star next to the state capital.
2. Label the bordering states.
3. Label three major cities.
4. Label the largest airport in the state.
5. Write three agricultural products that are grown in the state.
6. Write three major industries that are operated in the state.

C **ACADEMIC** **LET'S TALK.** As a group, present your research to your classmates.

TECHNOLOGY: YESTERDAY AND TODAY

Rotary phones were widely used until the 1980s.

AT WORK Identify and describe technology in the workplace; read and discuss workplace cellphone policies

ACADEMIC Recall key details; listen and record specific facts; make inferences using background knowledge; state reasons for opinions

CIVICS Read a consumer complaint email; write an email to local government expressing an opinion on a civic matter

1.

the insulin pump

Dean Kamen

1970s

2.

the compact fluorescent bulb

Ed Hammer

_____

3.

the electric car

William Morrison

_____

4.

the cellphone camera

Philippe Kahn

_____

5.

the artificial heart

Robert Jarvik

_____

6.

the laptop computer

William Moggridge

_____

7.

video games

Ralph Baer

_____

8.

the hepatitis B vaccine

Baruch Blumberg

_____

9.

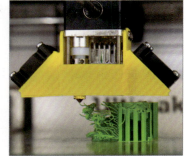

the 3-D printer

Charles Hull

_____

Subject	Be	Past Participle	
The insulin pump	was	invented	by Dean Kamen.
	was not		last year.
747 jumbo jets	were	designed	by Boeing engineers.
	were not		in the 1800s.

A Complete the information. Use the simple past passive.

1. The first compact fluorescent bulb (invent) _____ was invented _____ by a General Electric engineer named Ed Hammer. Hammer (assign) _____ to develop more energy-efficient bulbs in the mid-1970s, when there was an energy crisis in the US. Hammer worked for years. Finally, in 1976, the compact fluorescent bulb shape (create) _____. General Electric didn't sell the bulb at first because of production costs. Then, Hammer's design (discover) _____ by other companies, and it (copy) _____. Today, the bulbs (sell) _____ in all stores.

2. In June 1997, the first child of Philippe Kahn and his wife _____. Kahn wanted to send photos of their new child to their friends, so he connected his cellphone, digital camera, and laptop together. After the birth of the child, photos (email) _____ to many of his friends. The friends (shock) _____ by the instant photos that (send) _____. Soon after, Kahn started a technology company, and in 2005 it (sell) _____ for hundreds of millions of dollars.

B **ACADEMIC** Answer the questions in complete sentences. Use the simple past passive.

1. When was one of the first camera phones invented?
2. Why was it invented?
3. By whom was the artificial heart invented?
4. When was the hepatitis B vaccine developed?
5. Why was the fluorescent bulb created?
6. When was the first electric car developed in the US?
7. When was the 3-D printer invented?

Active	NASA **invented** the space shuttle.
Passive	The space shuttle **was invented** by NASA.

Active sentences usually emphasize the person or thing that does the action.
Passive sentences usually emphasize the person or thing that receives the action.

A Read the paragraph. Underline the passive verbs. Circle the active verbs.

The automobile <u>was developed</u> in the late 1800s, and in the early 1900s cars were already used in Europe and the United States on a limited basis. In 1908, Henry Ford (developed) a more affordable car. That car was called the Model T. The first moving assembly line was installed in his factory in 1913. This reduced the cost and time of producing a car. A Model T was assembled in 93 minutes and cost $850. By 1927, more than 15 million cars were on the roads in the United States.

B Circle *A* for active or *P* for passive.

1.	The first cars didn't have windshield wipers.	Ⓐ	P
2.	People got out of their cars to clean their windshields.	A	P
3.	The first windshield wipers were invented by Mary Anderson.	A	P
4.	They were operated from the inside of the car.	A	P
5.	Before 1929, people could not listen to the radio in their cars.	A	P
6.	The car radio was developed by Paul Galvin.	A	P
7.	The first car radios were not installed at the automobile factory.	A	P
8.	Car owners took their cars to a separate company for radio installation.	A	P
9.	Turn signals were installed in cars for consumers in 1939.	A	P
10.	Before this, people used their hands to signal a turn.	A	P

Ford Model T cars waiting to be delivered after leaving the assembly line in 1925.

C Complete the sentences. Use the passive or active form of the simple past.

1. J.P. Knight (develop) _____developed_____ the world's first traffic signal in London.

2. Before this, many people (kill) _____ in traffic accidents.

3. Two positions (feature) _____ on this new device: Go and Stop.
   A policeman (operate) _____ the device.

4. Unfortunately, the device (explode) _____ due to a gas leak and
   (injure) _____ a policeman who was operating it.

5. After that, Knight's traffic light (abandon) _____ because people
   were worried about its safety.

6. The first parking meters (install) _____ in Oklahoma City.

7. Some drivers (resist) _____ this change at first, but over time,
   parking meters (introduce) _____ in more and more cities.

8. The air bag (invent) _____ by John Hetrick in 1952.

9. Air bags (offer) _____ as an option in the 1973 Chevy Impala.

10. For many years, air bags (not / consider) _____ to be important.
    Now, they are standard equipment.

D **ACADEMIC** **LET'S TALK.** Talk with a partner about each advance in car and traffic technology.
Use the information in the chart below. What did people do before each item was invented?

> Windshield wipers were invented by Mary Anderson in 1903. Before that, drivers had to pull over to the side of the road and clean their windshields by hand.

WORD PARTNERSHIPS

parking	lot
	meter
	space
	spot

Invention	Inventor	Year
1. windshield wipers	Mary Anderson	1903
2. traffic light	J.P. Knight	1868
3. low-cost car radio	Paul Galvin	1930
4. GPS	US Department of Defense	1973
5. turn signals	Oscar Simler	1929
6. air-conditioning	Packard	1939
7. air bags	John Hetrick	1952

In past passive sentences, include the person or thing that did the action when it is important and not obvious. Use *by*.

Baruch Blumberg invented the hepatitis B vaccine.

The hepatitis B vaccine **was invented by Baruch Blumberg**.

When the person or thing that did the action is obvious, unimportant, or unknown, it does not need to be included.

Many years ago, hospitals did not sterilize medical equipment.

Many years ago, medical equipment **was not sterilized**.

A Rewrite the sentences. Use the passive voice. Include the person or thing that does the action and use *by* when necessary.

1. The Romans began the first hospitals.

   The first hospitals were begun by the Romans.

2. Doctors implanted the first artificial heart in Dr. Barney Clark in 1982.

   The first artificial heart was implanted in Dr. Barney Clark in 1982.

3. Sir Alexander Fleming discovered penicillin in 1928.

   _____

4. Doctors performed the first laser surgery to correct vision in 1987.

   _____

5. Ian McDonald invented ultrasound in 1958.

   _____

6. Dr. Christiaan Barnard performed the first heart transplant in Cape Town, South Africa.

   _____

7. The Federal Drug Administration (FDA) approved the hepatitis B vaccine in 1981.

   _____

8. Schools require students to have the hepatitis B vaccine.

   _____

9. Bernard Fantus established the first blood bank in the United States in 1937.

   _____

10. Doctors perform many operations on an outpatient basis.

    _____

B **Pronunciation: Compound Nouns** Listen and repeat. Use the correct stress. 🎧71

1. **tooth**paste
2. **air** conditioner
3. **lie** detector
4. **wash**ing machine
5. **co**py machine

6. **park**ing meter
7. **con**tact lenses
8. **seat** belt
9. **la**ser printer
10. **cell**phone

> A compound noun is a noun made up of two or more words. The first syllable of the first word in a compound noun is stressed.

C **AT WORK** **LET'S TALK.** List nine inventions you can find at work or in your classroom. Then, answer the questions about each one with a partner.

1. _____
2. _____
3. _____

4. _____
5. _____
6. _____

7. _____
8. _____
9. _____

1. What is the name of the invention?
2. How many years ago do you think it was invented?
3. What is it made of?
4. What is it used for?
5. What did people use before we had this invention?

> This invention is called a "projector." I think it was invented around 50 years ago. I think it's made of plastic, glass, and metal. It is used for showing words, photos, or videos on a large screen. Before this was invented, people wrote words or drew pictures on a board.

Projectors are often used to give presentations.

D Listen to the sentences and circle *Active* or *Passive*. 🎧72

1. (Active) Passive   4. Active Passive   7. Active Passive
2. Active Passive   5. Active Passive   8. Active Passive
3. Active Passive   6. Active Passive   9. Active Passive

E **ACADEMIC** Listen and complete the sentence that you hear. 🎧72

1. Two engineers _made the first call by cellphone_ _____.

2. One man called from New York City while the other _____ in New Jersey.

3. Software applications for electronic devices _____.

4. In 1994, _____ by IBM.

5. Clock, calendar, _____ on one of the first smartphones.

6. Throughout the 90's, _____.

7. Today, _____ every month.

8. Americans ages 18 to 24 _____.

9. Many of the most popular apps _____.

F Complete the sentences about one of your favorite smartphone apps. Use the active or passive form of the simple present or simple past.

1. One of my favorite apps (call) _____

   _____.
       app name

2. It (design) _____ by _____.

3. I (download) _____ this app _____ **days / months / years** ago.

4. I access this app _____ a **day / month / year**.

5. This app (use) _____ for _____

   _____.

G **LET'S TALK.** In groups, discuss the app that you selected in Exercise F.

ACTIVE GRAMMAR / Other Passive Forms

Simple present	Air bags **are installed** in all cars.
Present continuous	Those cars **are being repaired**.
Simple past	Air bags **were installed** in 1973.
Past continuous	My car **was being repaired** while I was waiting.
Future with *will*	A new model **will be delivered** tomorrow.
Future with *be going to*	That car **is going to be inspected** tomorrow.
Present perfect simple	Many changes **have been made** to today's cars.

All passive verbs use a form of the verb *to be* + the past participle.

A Complete the sentences. Use the correct passive form.

1. The first personal computer (call) _____ was called _____ the MITS Altair 8800.

2. I believe that future cars (power) _____ by solar panels.

3. My textbook (download) _____ on my phone right now.

4. The first hybrid car (manufacture) _____ in the early 20th century.

5. More electric cars (drive) _____ on the West Coast than on the East Coast.

6. I think cheaper robots for households (design) _____ by 2050.

7. Some inventions (discover) _____ by mistake.

8. Many diabetics' lives (change) _____ by the invention of the insulin pump.

9. When (deliver) _____ packages _____ by drones?

10. (invent) _____ flying cars _____ yet?

A Listen and point to each picture of shopping technology. 🎧73

B ACADEMIC Listen again and complete the chart. 🎧73

Invention	Date	Invention	Date
1. the catalog	1872	**4.** the credit card	
2. the cash register		**5.** the barcode (UPC)	
3. the shopping cart		**6.** online shopping	

C ACADEMIC Listen a third time and take notes in your notebook. How did each invention help people? Compare your information with your classmates. 🎧73

D **ACADEMIC** Read the descriptions and write the names of the inventions.

1. Before this invention, all receipts were handwritten. _____the cash register_____

2. This invention was created in 1973. _____

3. With this advance in technology, it's easy to compare prices. _____

4. This idea was developed by a traveling salesman. _____

5. This invention was designed by a grocery store owner. _____

6. This invention was first used by business travelers. _____

E **ACADEMIC** Answer the questions.

1. Why were traveling salesmen necessary?

2. How did Aaron Montgomery Ward travel?

3. Where did store owners keep their money before 1884?

4. How did the cash register make shopping simpler?

5. Why did customers need shopping carts?

6. Who were the first credit card users?

7. What inventions do supermarket clerks use?

8. How do barcodes make supermarket clerks' jobs easier?

9. How can online shopping save customers money?

F Complete the sentences. Use the active or passive form of the simple present or simple past.

1. The first mail-order catalog (print) _____was printed_____ in 1872. Customers
   (look) _____ through the catalog and
   (order) _____ the items they wanted.

2. Before 1950, customers (pay) _____ for their purchases with cash or by
   check. The first credit cards (issue) _____ to business travelers. With a
   credit card, people (not / need)_____ to carry a lot of cash.

3. The first UPC scanner (install) _____ in a supermarket in Ohio.
   Today, supermarket clerks simply (scan) _____ each item. The price
   (appear) _____ on the cash register's screen.

READING / Informative Article

A **AT WORK** Discuss the questions.

1. Does your workplace or the workplace of a friend or family member have a cellphone policy?

2. Besides your home, what is a good place to use your cellphone?

B Match.

___c___ **1.** appropriate   **a.** the time and rate at which work is completed or products are produced

_____ **2.** enforcement   **b.** limited

_____ **3.** to institute   **c.** correct or good for a time or situation

_____ **4.** productivity   **d.** making sure people follow a rule or a law

_____ **5.** restricted   **e.** to start a new system, rule, or process

---

READING NOTE

Reading Long Passages

As you read a long passage, it is a good idea to summarize each paragraph in your notes. This will help you remember what you have read.

    <u>Summary of paragraph 1:</u> Many Americans agree on which places are appropriate for cellphone use.

C Read the text.

D **ACADEMIC** Circle *True* or *False*.

1. Most Americans think that using cellphones on the street is okay.	(True)	False
2. Most Americans do not use their cellphones at social events.	True	False
3. Most workers use their cellphones more than an hour a day at work.	True	False
4. Most employees do not watch sports while they're at work.	True	False
5. Younger workers use their devices more often than older workers.	True	False
6. Some policies require employees to put their phones in drawers.	True	False
7. All cellphone policies are the same.	True	False
8. Taking photos with cellphones is restricted in some workplaces.	True	False

Cellphones in the Workplace

The Pew Research Center, an organization that surveys the public on many issues, has asked Americans about their cellphone use and found some interesting results. 75% of American adults agree that using a cellphone on the street or on public transportation is acceptable. However, most agree that meetings, churches, and movie theaters are not **appropriate** places to use cellphones. The majority of the people surveyed reported that they used their cellphones at social events. How about in the workplace? Are workers allowed to use their cellphones while they are at work?

A survey by another organization reported that the average worker uses a cellphone for non-work-related activities 56 minutes per day. That equals approximately five hours a week. Most of that time, workers are browsing the internet and using social media. They spend less time playing games, shopping, and watching sports. Another survey discovered that 82 percent of employees keep their phones on their desks so that they can check for messages and texts, and 66 percent of workers use their cellphones several times a day. Who wastes the most time at work because of cellphones? Younger workers do. Workers 18 to 34 years old spend the most time on their mobile devices. Time spent on cellphones often decreases **productivity**, causing problems for many companies.

To prevent this loss of productivity, some companies have decided to **institute** specific policies on cellphone use. These policies range from simple advice to strict **enforcement** of the rules. Employees may have their cellphone use **restricted** to break times or certain areas other than the employees' desks or work stations. Other polices may restrict the length of calls to two or three minutes and require cellphones to be in silent mode and in a desk drawer. If an employee has to work with customers, that employee may have to keep their cellphone in a locker away from the work area. Workplaces like hospitals and government offices may have strict policies because of problems with security. An employee could even be fired for using a cellphone to take photos of patients or confidential papers.

What do you think? Is a cellphone policy necessary at every workplace? 🎧 74

Employees use cellphones in a workshop.

A **CIVICS** Read the email from a customer to a restaurant owner.

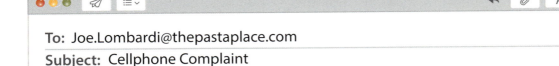

To: Joe.Lombardi@thepastaplace.com

Subject: Cellphone Complaint

Dear Mr. Lombardi,

My name is Teresa Santiago. My husband and I visited your restaurant this past Friday evening. During our meal, a woman at the next table received a call on her cellphone. Her loud conversation continued for twenty minutes. No one asked her to take the call outside. My husband and I were looking forward to a relaxing evening, a good dinner, and quiet conversation. We didn't pay $52 to listen to another customer's personal problems.

I'd like you to consider instituting a no-cellphone policy at your restaurant. Please follow the example of several other restaurants in the city that have posted signs saying, "Please limit cellphone usage," or "Cellphone use not permitted inside."

Sincerely,

Teresa Santiago

WRITING NOTE

A Letter Expressing an Opinion
1. Begin with *Dear Mr. / Ms.* (name) or *Dear Sir* or *Madam*.
2. State your problem. Be clear. State the reasons for your complaint.
3. End with *Sincerely*.
4. Type your full name.

B **ACADEMIC** Discuss the picture below with a partner. Is it safe to use a cellphone while driving? Write two more reasons under each opinion below.

Drivers should be allowed to use cellphones while driving:

1. _Drivers spend hours in traffic, and talking to friends helps them pass the time._

2. _____

3. _____

Drivers should not be allowed to use cellphones while driving:

1. _A person who is holding a cellphone can only have one hand on the wheel._

2. _____

3. _____

C **CIVICS** Your city is considering a ban on using cellphones in cars and in restaurants. Write a letter to your mayor. Express your opinion on this issue.

1. Begin the letter with a greeting and introduce yourself.

2. State your opinion, and then give two or three reasons.

3. End your letter appropriately.

D **ACADEMIC** Exchange letters with a partner. Answer the questions.

1. What is your partner's opinion?

2. What are your partner's reasons for their opinion?

E Find and correct the mistakes.

1. The accident was ~~causing~~ *caused* by a driver talking on a cellphone.

2. The driver distracted by her cellphone.

3. Yesterday I was seen an accident.

4. Olivia's parents were bought her wireless headphones for her cellphone.

5. He was gave a ticket for driving while using a cellphone.

A AT WORK **LET'S TALK.** Read the company's cellphone policy. Discuss the policy with a partner. Is it too strict, just right, or not strict enough?

Company Guidelines for Cellphone Use

The following are the cellphone use guidelines for all of our employees during the work day. The company does not permit cellphone use if it could be a risk to the company's security. Cellphones must not be used if they will cause an employee to **neglect** work responsibilities. Employees must not use a cellphone while driving.

- Do not use a cellphone while operating heavy equipment.
- Do not use cellphones for browsing the internet or playing games during work hours.
- Do not use work cellphones for personal business.
- Do not use cellphones during meetings.

Cellphones are appropriate in the following situations:

- It is necessary to make a work-related call.
- It is necessary to text or email a client for work-related business.
- It is necessary to keep a contact file of clients.
- It is necessary to check on an ill family member.

What happens in the case of inappropriate cellphone use?
If an employee has been warned about **inappropriate** cellphone use and continues to **violate** company policies, disciplinary action will be taken. If an employee uses a cellphone in a way that **endangers** the company or its employees, or is against the law, the employee may be **terminated**.

B Match.

__d__ **1.** neglect	**a.** not correct or good for a time or situation
_____ **2.** inappropriate	**b.** put in danger of being hurt
_____ **3.** violate	**c.** fired, or dismissed from a job
_____ **4.** endanger	**d.** pay very little attention to
_____ **5.** terminated	**e.** disobey or go against a law or rule

C **LET'S TALK.** Work in a group. Write a cellphone policy for your class or school. Share the policy with the class.

UNIT 13 MUSIC

AT WORK Write sentences about work history; read and construct a timeline of professional experiences

ACADEMIC Identify grammatical patterns; differentiate between word forms; check texts for errors; prepare and give a research-based presentation

CIVICS Discuss and identify aspects of American history and culture

A trumpet player in a mariachi band.

A LET'S TALK. Work with a partner. Discuss the types of music in the box below. Then, match each photo with a type of music.

~~classical~~	heavy metal	jazz	pop	rock
country	hip-hop	opera	reggae	salsa

1.

classical

4.

_____

2.

_____

5.

_____

3.

_____

6.

_____

B Discuss the questions.

1. What's your favorite kind of music? Why?

2. Who is your favorite artist? Why?

3. Do you play an instrument? If so, what do you play?

/ Relative Clauses with *Who* and *Which*

A relative clause describes or gives more information about a noun. Relative clauses can begin with relative pronouns such as *who* and *which*.

Who introduces information about a person.

<u>My father</u>, **who used to play in a band**, is now a high school music teacher.

Which introduces information about a place or thing.

The music for <u>*West Side Story*</u>, **which was both a Broadway musical and a movie**, was written by Leonard Bernstein.

A **ACADEMIC** Read and complete each relative clause with *who* or *which*.

1. Our orchestra's conductor, _____*who*_____ is from California, holds practices two times a week.

2. The saxophone, _____ is a brass instrument, is often used in jazz music.

3. My piano teacher, _____ is originally from Russia, plays the piano beautifully.

4. His youngest cousin, _____ is now a solar panel salesman, used to play drums in a band.

5. We played in our high school marching band, _____ performed at all of the football games.

6. Lisa plays the violin, _____ is a difficult instrument to learn.

7. The band's lead singer, _____ is only seventeen, will graduate from high school this year.

8. Many famous musicians have attended the Berklee School of Music, _____ has connections with the Boston Symphony Orchestra.

9. Lincoln Center, _____ is located near Central Park, has more than one theater.

10. Kristin, _____ has a beautiful voice, is planning to major in musical theater.

The Boston Symphony Orchestra.

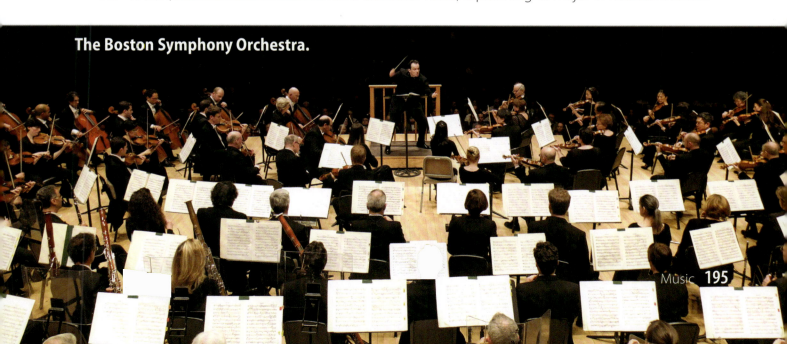

Relative clauses can also begin with the relative pronouns *whom* and *whose*.

Whom introduces information about a person; this person must be the object of the relative clause.

She's writing a song for her son. She named her son after her father.

She's writing a song for <u>her son</u>, **whom she named after her father**.

Whose acts as a possessive form in the relative clause; a noun always follows *whose*.

John Lennon is still famous today. <u>His</u> wife and sons also have musical talent.

John Lennon, **whose wife and sons also have musical talent**, is still famous today.

A **ACADEMIC** Read and complete each relative clause with *whom* or *whose*.

1. Last year, I visited Carnegie Hall with my brother, _____*whose*_____ friend was performing with an orchestra.

2. The middle school students performed with their teachers, _____ they greatly admire.

3. Victor lent a guitar to his brother, _____ instrument needed repairs.

4. Mark and Vanessa, _____ I saw perform last summer, are going to play at the city auditorium next weekend.

5. Joy, _____ mother was a concert pianist, decided to take drum lessons.

6. My favorite songwriter, _____ I have admired for a long time, has finally produced her own album.

B Complete the clauses with the information from the box below.

~~career spanned five decades~~	many pop singers have performed with	R&B group was a big hit
is located in Tennessee	originated in New York City	

1. Celia Cruz, whose _____*career spanned five decades*_____, earned many music awards and medals.

2. Nashville, which _____, is known as Music City.

3. Hip-hop, which _____, is a combination of music, fashion, and culture.

4. Andrea Bocelli, whom _____, has successfully put classical music on the pop charts.

5. Beyoncé, whose _____, has been a successful solo artist since 2003.

C Answer the questions about your classmates.

1. Who do you sit next to in class? _____

2. Who has been in this country for two years or more? _____

3. Who has a difficult work schedule? _____

4. Who has long hair? _____

5. Who often listens to music before class begins? _____

D Work in groups. Complete the sentences. Use the information from Exercise C.

_____Beata_____, whom _____I sit next to_____,
　　　　　name of student

is from _____Poland_____.
　　　　　　　　　　　native country

1. _____, who _____sits next to me_____,
　　　　　name of student

is from _____.
　　　　　　　　　　　native country

2. _____, whom _____,
　　　　　name of student

is from _____.
　　　　　　　　　　　native country

3. _____, who _____,
　　　　　name of student

is from _____.
　　　　　　　　　　　native country

4. _____, whose _____,
　　　　　name of student

is from _____.
　　　　　　　　　　　native country

5. _____, who _____,
　　　　　name of student

is from _____.
　　　　　　　　　　　native country

E In your notebook, write five more sentences about your classmates. Include relative clauses that begin with *who*, *which*, *whom*, or *whose*.

There are two types of relative clauses: non-restrictive and restrictive. A non-restrictive clause gives extra, or non-essential, information about a noun. Commas are used to separate a non-restrictive clause from a main clause. *Which* is only used with non-restrictive clauses.

We paid <u>Dave Jones</u>, **whom we hired to sing at our wedding**.

(Meaning: We know who Dave Jones is. The relative clause gives extra information about Dave Jones.)

<u>Radio City Music Hall</u>, **which was opened in 1932**, can hold 6,015 people.

(Meaning: We know Radio City Music Hall. The relative clause gives extra information about it.)

A restrictive clause gives essential information about the noun it describes. Commas are *not* used with restrictive clauses.

<u>The students</u> **who studied at Juilliard** were great musicians.

(Meaning: We do not know who the students are without the clause. The clause is necessary.)

The relative pronoun *that* can be used in restrictive clauses to replace *who* or *whom* in casual speech. This is not acceptable in academic writing.

<u>The man</u> **that we hired to sing at our wedding** was very talented.

A **ACADEMIC** Read the sentences. Write *R* if the relative clause is restrictive and *NR* if the relative clause is non-restrictive.

_____R_____ **1.** I've just listened to the album that I downloaded.

_____ **2.** The erhu, which is sometimes called the Chinese violin, is a two-stringed instrument played with a bow.

_____ **3.** The new music-streaming service that I use is free.

_____ **4.** My living room speakers, which are next to the TV, are connected to my home system.

_____ **5.** The singer who is from Florida won the competition.

_____ **6.** One of my favorite songs, which I've been listening to every day, is number one this week.

_____ **7.** The couple hired a DJ that plays music at many local weddings.

_____ **8.** The youth orchestra that my niece belongs to played at Carnegie Hall last month.

_____ **9.** The first Broadway show, which was named "The Black Crook," was performed in 1866.

_____**10.** My sister, who graduated from Juilliard, is a professional singer now.

B Listen. Then, answer the questions with a partner. 🎧 **75**

1. What is the grandson listening to?

2. What are the grandmother and grandson talking about?

3. How did the grandmother listen to music when she was younger?

4. What was inconvenient about 45s and LPs?

5. What do some people think about LPs?

6. What does the grandmother have in the basement?

7. What are they going to do next?

8. Have you ever listened to 45s or LPs?

C Match the technology to the correct description.

_____*c*_____ **1.** earbuds	**a.** a machine / plays 45s and LPs
_____ **2.** a cellphone	**b.** a record / plays an entire full-length album
_____ **3.** streaming	**c.** devices / you insert into your ears
_____ **4.** an LP	**d.** a record / plays one or two songs on each side
_____ **5.** a 45	**e.** a way of playing music / uses the internet
_____ **6.** a turntable	**f.** a device / is like a computer

D **LET'S TALK.** With a partner, ask and answer questions about the technology listed in Exercise C. Use *that*.

> What are earbuds?

> They're devices that you insert into your ears to listen to music.

Relative clauses can also begin with *when* and *where*.
When introduces information about a time. **Where** introduces information about a place.
Both *when* and *where* can be used with non-restrictive and restrictive clauses.
 Carnegie Hall is located in <u>Midtown Manhattan</u>, **where it was built in 1890**.
 It opened in <u>an era</u> **when the neighborhood was not used to such a large building**.

A Read the text. Then, complete the sentences about Carnegie Hall.

 Carnegie Hall is located in Midtown Manhattan. Classical and popular music are performed there. In 1928, "An American in Paris" debuted there. In 1964, Carnegie Hall became a US National Historic Landmark. Around 700 events are held there each season.

1. Midtown Manhattan is the area where _____ *Carnegie Hall is located* _____.

2. Carnegie Hall is a music hall where _____.

3. 1928 is the year when _____ at Carnegie Hall.

4. _____ is the year when Carnegie Hall _____.

5. _____ is a place where _____.

B **AT WORK** Complete the sentences about your work history. Use *where* and *when*.

1. _____ is the place where _____ *I had my first job* _____.

2. I attended _____, where I _____.

3. _____ is the year _____.

4. _____ is the place _____.

5. _____ is the time _____.

Carnegie Hall.

ACTIVE GRAMMAR | Review of Relative Clauses

A Complete the sentences about your musical preferences.

1. _____ is my favorite musician.

2. _____ is my favorite type of music.

3. _____ is my favorite musical group.

4. _____ is my favorite American singer.

5. _____ is my favorite radio station.

6. _____ is my favorite place to go dancing.

B Write sentences about your preferences in Exercise A. Use relative clauses with *who*, *which*, *whom*, *whose*, *that*, *when*, or *where*. Then, discuss your preferences with a partner.

1. John Legend, who is my favorite musician, is from Ohio.

2. _____

3. _____

4. _____

5. _____

6. _____

C **LET'S TALK.** Complete the questions. Then, ask and answer the questions with a partner.

> Do you know a store where I can buy good speakers?

> Yes, I do. You should try Tech Stop on Broad Street.

1. Do you know a dance club where _____?

2. Do you know a concert hall where _____?

3. Do you know a(n) _____?

4. Do you know a(n) _____?

5. Do you know a(n) _____?

6. Do you know a(n) _____?

A **CIVICS** Discuss the questions.

1. Look at the picture. Have you ever heard these instruments?
2. What state is labeled on the map? What do you know about this state?
3. What countries are labeled on the map?

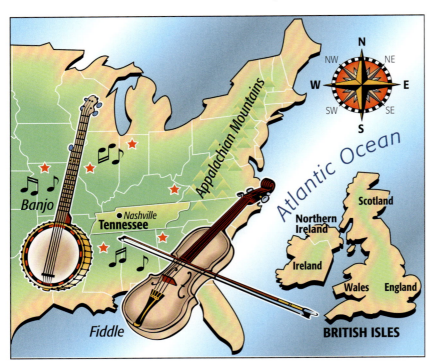

B **CIVICS** Listen to the information about the history of country music. Then, circle *T* for *True* or *F* for *False*. 🎧 76

1. The people living in the Appalachian Mountains were the first people to make country music in the US.   (T)   F

2. Music was not important to the people of the Appalachian Mountains.   T   F

3. Ballads were often happy songs.   T   F

4. African American music was important to the development of country music.   T   F

5. The banjo, which became popular among country musicians, came from South America.   T   F

6. The fiddle was one of the main instruments of country music.   T   F

7. The first superstars of country music recorded in 1947.   T   F

8. Jimmie Rodgers and the Carter Family became the first superstars of country music.   T   F

C **CIVICS** Listen again. With a partner, ask and answer the questions. 🎧76

1. How long ago did country music appear in the Appalachian Mountains?

2. How were the people from the United States and the British Isles similar?

3. What kinds of songs did the immigrants from the British Isles bring to the US?

4. What kind of instruments did country musicians use?

5. Where did the banjo originate from?

6. Which musician played the melody of most country songs?

7. Besides the banjo and fiddle, what other instruments are used in country music today?

8. In what year did Jimmie Rodgers and the Carter Family first record?

D Complete the sentences. Use a relative pronoun from the box. Some pronouns will be used more than once.

that	when	where	which	who	whom	whose

1. Some elements of country music originated from the British Isles, _____which_____ include Scotland, Ireland, Northern Ireland, England, and Wales.

2. Today's country music began in the Appalachian Mountains, _____ the music could be found from the northeast to the south.

3. Music was important to the Appalachian people, _____ often sang while working or attending community events.

4. The immigrants _____ came from the British Isles usually spoke English as their native language.

5. Ballads were songs _____ often told sad stories of love or war.

6. The banjo was brought to this country from Africa at a time _____ slavery was legal.

7. The fiddler, _____ instrument became very popular in country music, was often the leader of community dances.

8. Electric guitars and keyboards, _____ are popular instruments in country music today, weren't used in early country songs.

9. Jimmie Rodgers and the Carter Family, _____ a Virginia record company first recorded in 1927, were the earliest superstars of country music.

Music and New Orleans

The history of New Orleans is different from the history of many other US cities. The city was founded in 1718 by the French. Starting in 1763, the city was governed by the Spanish. In 1803, the Louisiana territories were again controlled by France, but they were quickly sold to the United States in a transaction called the Louisiana Purchase.

New Orleans began with a French-speaking **culture** that included a love of good food, wine, music, and dancing. Later, Africans, some free and some slaves, arrived in the city and brought West Indian culture from the Caribbean. French, Spanish, and African/Caribbean cultures mixed to create a new language and culture called Creole. After that, African Americans from around the US moved to New Orleans, adding yet another **cultural** and **musical** element to the city.

Jazz music began in the African American communities, but it was also influenced by the ethnic diversity of New Orleans. Bands, which were led by brass instruments such as trumpets and trombones, participated in many community events like parades and even funeral processions. **Music** was a part of every celebration.

In the late 1800s, some **musicians** started improvising, or changing the music and making up new melodies as they played. This was also a time when the Creole and African American musicians began to combine their styles. In the early 1900s, the **popularity** of jazz spread to other cities, especially to clubs in Chicago and New York City.

Louis Armstrong (1901–1971), who was a very **popular** jazz musician, was born in New Orleans. During the 1920s, Armstrong developed his style as a solo artist, but his recordings with his bands, which were called the Hot Five and the Hot Seven, made him an international star. He toured continuously until he died in 1971.

After Hurricane Katrina hit New Orleans in 2005, many musicians lost their homes and had to leave the city. Two New Orleans musicians, Harry Connick Jr. and Branford Marsalis, raised money to build the Musicians' Village. This community includes 77 homes and a music center where people can learn, listen to, dance to, and produce music. 🔊77

The Treme Brass Band performs at the Candlelight Lounge in the Treme neighborhood of New Orleans.

A CIVICS Discuss the questions. Then, read the text.

1. What do you know about New Orleans?

2. Look at the photo on the previous page. What kind of music do you think they are playing?

B **CIVICS** Complete the sentences.

1. _____ France _____ was the first country to govern New Orleans.

2. Examples of brass instruments are trumpets and _____.

3. Music was played at _____ processions and parades.

4. Creole is a mix of _____, Spanish, and African cultures.

5. _____ means that a musician makes original changes to the music while he or she is playing.

6. _____ became an international star.

7. The Musicians' Village includes _____.

READING NOTE

Recognizing Word Forms

When you study vocabulary, it is important to recognize different word forms so that you can use the words correctly.

Noun:	culture	music / musician	popularity
Adjective:	cultural	musical	popular

C **ACADEMIC** Circle the correct word forms.

1. The **culture** / **cultural** of New Orleans is different from that of other US cities.

2. New Orleans' **music** / **musical** is a big part of the city's culture.

3. Jazz became **popularity** / **popular** in major cities like Chicago and New York.

4. One **culture** / **cultural** tradition in New Orleans is the funeral procession.

5. Louis Armstrong helped spread the **popularity** / **popular** of jazz.

6. The different ethnic groups helped create a different **music** / **musical** form.

D **▶ WATCH** This video is about an important New Orleans holiday called Mardi Gras. Choose a Mardi Gras topic from the box below. Then, watch the video and take notes on this topic. Discuss your notes with classmates who chose the same topic. Then, share your notes with the class.

costumes	floats	food	music

A Mardi Gras float.

A **AT WORK** Read the timeline of Leonard Bernstein's life.

1918	Born in Lawrence, Massachusetts
1931	Became very good at the piano; his father bought him a baby grand piano
1937	Met the conductor of the Boston Symphony Orchestra
1939	Graduated from Harvard University; didn't serve in World War II; had asthma
1940	Accepted into master conducting class at Berkshire Music Center at Tanglewood
1943	Became assistant conductor of the New York Philharmonic; substituted for conductor; received excellent reviews in the <u>New York Times</u>
1945–1947	Conducted New York City Center orchestra; guest conductor in many cities
1951	Got married
1956	Wrote the operetta, *Candide*
1957	Premiered *West Side Story*
1958–1980	Televised 53 Young People's Concerts to teach children about music; moved the Philharmonic to Lincoln Center; received honors from the Kennedy Center
1982	Served as artistic director at the Los Angeles Philharmonic Institute
1990	Died in New York City

B Read the biography.

Leonard Bernstein was born in Lawrence, Massachusetts. His father was from Ukraine. When Bernstein was ten years old, he saved his own money to pay for piano lessons. He became very good, so his father bought him a baby grand piano. Bernstein graduated from Boston Latin School and Harvard University, where he studied music theory. In 1937, he met the conductor of the Boston Symphony Orchestra (BSO), and in 1940, he was accepted into a master conducting class at Tanglewood, which was the BSO's summer home. During World War II, Bernstein became assistant conductor of the New York Philharmonic while many other musicians were serving in the war. When the conductor became ill, Bernstein substituted and received excellent reviews in the <u>New York Times</u>. In 1951, he got married. In 1956, he wrote the operetta, *Candide*, and the next year, he collaborated on *West Side Story*, which made him even more popular. Bernstein enjoyed teaching and televised 53 Young People's Concerts. During the following years, he moved the Philharmonic to Lincoln Center, received honors from the Kennedy Center, and served as artistic director at the Los Angeles Philharmonic Institute. He died at age 72.

C **AT WORK** Make a timeline. Choose six to ten professionally significant events in your life or in the life of a family member. Write the year and a phrase about each event on a timeline.

> **WRITING NOTE**
>
> **Run-on Sentences**
> A run-on sentence is a long sentence that may have missing or incorrect punctuation. It may also overuse the word *and* or other conjunctions.
> **Run-on sentence:** The CMA Music Festival has been held for many years it attracts fans from all over the world.
> **Correct:** The CMA Music Festival has been held for many years**, and** it attracts fans from all over the world.

D **ACADEMIC** In your notebook, use the information in your timeline to write a biography or autobiography. Use two or more relative clauses. After you finish your paper, check for run-on sentences.

E **ACADEMIC** Exchange papers with a partner. Answer the questions.

1. What significant events did your partner describe?

2. What events interested you the most?

3. Does your partner's text have any run-on sentences?

F **ACADEMIC** Find and correct the mistakes.

1. The singer ~~who his~~ *whose* music I like has written many hit songs.

2. The Beatles toured all over the United States, and they went to New York City, and they were very popular.

3. The person whose is performing there has always been my favorite singer.

4. Louis Armstrong, was born in New Orleans, played the trumpet.

5. Leonard Bernstein conducted the New York Philharmonic, that moved to Lincoln Center.

6. The music festival lasts for four days is located in downtown Nashville.

7. The tickets for the concert where I am attending were more expensive than I expected.

Lincoln Center, home of the New York Philharmonic Orchestra.

A **ACADEMIC** You are going to give a presentation about a famous musician, member of a musical group, or music producer. Work with a partner. Go online and search for information about the person you want to present to your class. Type the person's name and "bio" in the search area. Find out the following information:

1. What is the person's original or given name?
2. Where was the person born?
3. Did this person grow up in a musical family? What was the family like?
4. What kind of music is the person known for?
5. How did the person get started in a music career?
6. What is the name of the person's first hit song?
7. What other success has the person had in their career?
8. What are four more interesting facts about the person?

WORD PARTNERSHIPS	
a hit	song
a popular	

B **ACADEMIC** Read the suggestions for making a presentation.

1. Show a picture of the person you're presenting.
2. Go online and find a song or part of a song that you can play for the class.
3. Before your presentation, check the pronunciation of any new words with your teacher.
4. Practice your presentation with your partner. Time yourselves.

C **ACADEMIC** With your partner, prepare a five- to seven-minute presentation about the performer you researched. Present your information to the class.

Student 1: Present the information in 1–3 of Exercise A as well as two interesting facts.

Student 2: Present the information in 4–7 of Exercise A as well as two interesting facts.

Congolese singer Jupiter Bokondji performs at GlobalFest in New York City.

BECOMING A CITIZEN

AT WORK Express opinions about finding a job; discuss the order of career steps

ACADEMIC Identify and apply grammatical rules; scan a text for errors; understand and apply test-taking strategies

CIVICS Understand the US citizenship process; discuss political platforms and campaigns; construct opinions on community issues; recall key information about American history and government

Two large beams of light shine behind the Statue of Liberty to commemorate the anniversary of September 11.

A Discuss the questions.

1. Are you a United States citizen? Is anyone in your family a citizen?

2. What are the benefits of becoming a citizen?

B **LET'S TALK.** With a partner, look at the pictures and guess what is happening in each one. Then, listen to Marco and Luciana's story about becoming United States citizens. Were your guesses correct? 🎧78

1.

2.

3.

4.

5.

6.

C **CIVICS** Read.

The Naturalization Process

1. Fill out the application.
2. Send the application, copies of requested documents, and payment of fees to your regional United States Citizenship and Immigration Service (USCIS) office. Send your application via certified mail.
3. Get and send copies of your fingerprints.
4. Go for your interview and naturalization test.
5. Take the oath of allegiance to the United States at your swearing-in ceremony.

CULTURE NOTE

The naturalization test is required for anyone who wants to become a US citizen. A USCIS examiner asks a citizenship applicant a group of questions from a list of 100 questions about US history and government.

When two verbs are used together, the second verb is often an infinitive. An infinitive is *to* + the base form of the verb.

> I **plan** *to become* a US citizen.
> Luciana **prepared** *to take* the naturalization test.

We can use an infinitive after the following verbs:

afford	forget	manage	remember
agree	hate	need	seem
ask	hope	offer	try
be able	intend	plan	volunteer
choose	know how	prefer	wait
decide	learn (how)	prepare	want
expect	like	promise	wish
fail	love	refuse	would like

A Listen and complete each sentence with the infinitive you hear. 🎧 79

1. Marco and Luciana wanted _____ *to become* _____ citizens.

2. They agreed _____ time after work preparing for the test.

3. They tried _____ the test questions as often as possible.

4. Their children promised _____ more with the household chores.

5. Marco already knew how _____ English well.

6. Luciana needed _____ English more.

7. She decided _____ an English course two days a week.

8. When they become citizens, they would like _____ to vote.

B Ask your teacher the questions.

1. Why did you decide to become a teacher?
2. Do you know how to speak another language?
3. Would you like to learn my native language?
4. Do you want to teach English in another country?
5. Where would you like to travel?
6. What do you like to do in your free time?
7. Do you know how to cook any ethnic foods?
8. Would you agree to end class early today?

Sadya Roble, an immigrant from Somalia, became a US citizen at a ceremony in Maine.

ACTIVE GRAMMAR   Verb + Object + Infinitive

> An object or object pronoun + an infinitive can be used after the following verbs:
>
> | | | | |
> |---|---|---|---|
> | advise | encourage | hire | remind | urge |
> | allow | expect | invite | require | want |
> | ask | forbid | permit | teach | warn |
> | convince | help | persuade | tell | |
>
> My supervisor **expects me *to use*** English with all of the customers.
> For negative sentences, place *not* before the infinitive.
> The interviewer **reminded us <u>not</u> *to arrive*** late to the ceremony.

A Restate each comment using an infinitive. Use the simple past form of the verb in parentheses.

1. The teacher said to us, "Fill out the information." (tell)

    > The teacher told us to fill out the information.

2. The teacher said to the students, "Don't come late to class." (warn)

3. A student asked me, "Why don't you make a study group?" (encourage)

4. The teacher said to the students, "Bring paper and your books every day." (expect)

5. The teacher said to us, "Yes, you can take a short break." (allow)

6. The teacher said to the students, "Don't forget your workbooks." (remind)

7. The teacher said to us, "Don't translate everything." (urge)

8. The teacher said to the students, "Please come to the school party." (invited)

B **ACADEMIC** Complete the sentences about Manika and her family. She is starting college, and her parents are about to leave. Use your imagination.

1. Manika's family helped her to _unpack her things_.

2. Manika's father is telling her to _____

    _____

3. Her mother is reminding her to _____.

4. Her parents allowed _____.

5. Manika's sister asked _____.

6. Manika's sister doesn't want _____.

7. Manika's parents expect _____.

ACTIVE GRAMMAR | *Be* + Adjective + Infinitive

The infinitive form can be used after the following adjectives:				
dangerous	good	important	polite	selfish
difficult	hard	impossible	possible	stressful
easy	healthy	interesting	reasonable	terrible
expensive	helpful	necessary	romantic	wonderful

It's **stressful *to move*** to a new country.

A **Pronunciation: Word Stress** Listen and underline the stressed syllable in each word. 🎧 80

1. <u>dan</u> • ger • ous

2. nec • es • sar • y

3. im • pos • si • ble

4. won • der • ful

5. po • lite

6. rea • son • a • ble

7. ro • man • tic

8. stress • ful

9. help • ful

B **ACADEMIC** Read the tips for studying for the naturalization test. Then, underline the adjectives and circle the infinitives.

It's <u>important</u> (to take) note of your naturalization interview date because it's difficult to reschedule if you need to miss it. It's impossible to study for the test in one day, so it's necessary to schedule your study time. There are different parts of the test (English reading, writing, speaking, and civics), so it's helpful to plan your study time for each section. Some parts may be easy to complete, but others may be more difficult to do. Good luck!

C **AT WORK** **LET'S TALK.** With a partner, use the chart to make sentences about your daily lives.

It's difficult It's easy It's expensive It's hard It's necessary It's stressful	to	arrive to class on time. buy a house in this country. find a decent job. find a good place to live. find time to exercise. get a job with benefits. get help with my homework. learn English grammar. make new friends in a new country. work full time and go to school.

> It's difficult to find time to exercise.

> When two verbs are used together, the second verb can also be a gerund.
> A gerund is a verb + *ing*. Gerunds can be used after the following verbs:
>
> | | | | | |
> |---|---|---|---|---|
> | admit | can't help | discuss | miss | recall |
> | anticipate | can't stand | enjoy | postpone | recommend |
> | appreciate | consider | imagine | practice | regret |
> | avoid | delay | mind | quit | stop |
>
> They **missed** *seeing* their family during the holidays.
> For negative sentences, place *not* before the gerund.
> She **regretted** <u>**not**</u> *visiting* her family more often.

A Listen and complete each sentence with the gerund you hear. 🎧 81

1. Many immigrants discuss _____ *becoming* _____ citizens.

2. Sometimes, they delay _____ the process because they are very busy.

3. People often regret _____ English classes before they immigrated.

4. Many immigrants anticipated _____ an easy time when they arrived.

5. Immigrants from tropical countries often can't imagine _____ heavy coats and sweaters.

6. Some people postpone _____ English until after their children finish school.

7. Many immigrant students don't mind _____ classes in the evening.

8. Some immigrants enjoy _____ about US history.

B Complete the sentences using the gerund form of the verbs in the box. Then, say the sentences aloud.

enroll	give	~~leave~~	speak	study

1. People usually discuss _____ *leaving* _____ their countries for many years before making a final decision.

2. Many immigrants anticipate _____ a better life to their children.

3. Some consider _____ a different field such as nursing or business.

4. Some immigrants can practice _____ English with their coworkers.

5. Some avoid _____ in English classes for many years.

C LET'S TALK. Work in groups. Practice the conversation. Then, talk about your preparations for coming to the United States using gerunds and the verbs listed on the previous page.

A: I began learning English before I came here. How about you?

B: No, I didn't study English. I regret not taking classes before I left.

C: I continued working until a few days before I left.

B: Me, too. I couldn't stop working.

D Complete the sentences about your experiences in the US. Use gerunds. Then, read your sentences to a partner.

1. When I came here, I appreciated _____.

2. When I first arrived, I enjoyed _____.

3. After some time, I regretted _____.

4. My friends recommended _____.

5. I can't help (worry) _____ about _____.

6. Now, I enjoy _____.

E What do you like about life in the United States? What don't you like? Write two or three gerunds in each column.

enjoy	don't mind	dislike / don't like	can't stand

F **ACADEMIC** **LET'S TALK.** In groups, compare your information from Exercise E.

A: I **can't stand** *wearing* a winter coat, hat, and gloves.

B: Why?

A: I come from a tropical country. I **don't like** *putting on* heavy clothing.

A snowstorm in New York City.

Gerunds can be used in time clauses with *after*, *before*, or *while* if the subject is the same in both the time clause and the main clause.

> **After Maria studied** for the naturalization test, she passed easily.
>
> **After *studying*** for the naturalization test, Maria passed easily.
>
> I studied for my English exam **while I was waiting** for my interview.
>
> I studied for my English exam **while *waiting*** for my interview.

A gerund can also be used after *in addition to*, *instead of*, or *without*.

> Many immigrants take a citizenship class **in addition to *working***.

A **AT WORK** Read the timeline of Paul's activities from 2004–2018. Then, complete the sentences.

2004 – applied for a visa

2007 – received his visa

2008 – arrived in the United States

2009 – began to study English; worked as a taxi driver

2012 – got a job at an auto body repair garage

2015 – applied for citizenship

2017 – became a citizen

2018 – got married; opened his own garage

1. After _____ waiting _____ for three years, Paul _____ received _____ his visa.

2. Instead of _____ English in Poland, Paul waited until he _____ in the United States.

3. He _____ as a taxi driver in addition to _____ an English class.

4. After _____ English for a couple of years, Paul _____ a different job.

5. It was difficult to open his own garage without _____ a citizen.

6. Paul had many documents to get before _____ for citizenship.

7. Instead of _____ earlier, he waited until after he was a citizen to marry his girlfriend.

B **AT WORK** Write three more sentences about Paul's life in your notebook. Use gerunds and the prepositions or prepositional phrases listed in the grammar box above.

> Gerunds can be used after the following verb + preposition phrases:
>
> | | | | |
> |---|---|---|---|
> | adjust to | complain about | plan on | tire of |
> | believe in | dream about | talk about | worry about |
> | care about | look forward to | think about | |
>
> When Paul lived in Poland, he **dreamed about** *moving* to the United States.

C Complete the sentences using gerunds. Then, read your sentences to a partner.

Before coming to the United States,…

1. I dreamed about _____.

2. I looked forward to _____.

After coming to the United States,…

3. I often talk about _____.

4. I often complain about _____.

> It was **impossible** *to find* a job in my country.
> My friends **didn't encourage me** *to speak* English.
> He **enjoyed** *working* at the real estate office.
> **After** *working* for a few years at a factory, I found another job.

D ACADEMIC Complete the sentences. Use the gerund or infinitive form of the verb.

1. It was impossible (find) _____ *to find* _____ a job in my country.

2. I have missed (see) _____ *seeing* _____ my family and friends.

3. I intend (visit) _____ my native country next year.

4. I expect my cousin (arrive) _____ soon.

5. Have you ever considered (become) _____ a citizen?

6. How long do you plan on (stay) _____ in this country?

7. It is difficult (learn) _____ another language.

8. My parents appreciated (receive) _____ a check from me each month.

9. It's expensive (get) _____ health insurance.

10. My cousin complains about (drive) _____ in heavy traffic.

A **CIVICS** Discuss the questions.

1. Look at the picture. What are the people doing?

2. The blond man in the picture is running for the city council. Describe local elections in your country. What happens during the campaign?

B **CIVICS** Listen. Then, retell the story about the local political campaign with a partner. 🎧82

C Listen again and circle *True* or *False*. 🎧82

1.	Erik is a US citizen.	(True)	False
2.	Erik has always been involved in politics.	True	False
3.	Erik used to vote in every election.	True	False
4.	Erik owns a bookstore and volunteers at an adult school.	True	False
5.	Erik hires senior citizens for this bookstore.	True	False
6.	Erik is running for the city council.	True	False
7.	Erik's wife, Andrea, is helping with the campaign.	True	False
8.	Erik has to spend a lot of money on the campaign.	True	False

D Complete the sentences.

give	have	make	organize	set	speak	spend	~~work~~

1. Erik enjoys _____ working _____ with students at the adult school.

2. Recently, Erik has been looking forward to _____ interviews.

3. Andrea is good at _____ people.

4. Volunteers have been talking about _____ a voter registration drive.

5. They're planning on _____ up registration tables at the supermarkets.

6. Erik's children and their friends enjoy _____ signs.

7. Erik is not worried about _____ too much money.

8. At first, Erik was worried about _____ in front of so many people.

E **ACADEMIC** Ask and answer questions about the story with a partner. Answer using the words in the box. One word will be used more than once.

Andrea	Erik	friends	Manuel	volunteers

1. who / enjoy / work with students

2. who / persuade Erik / run for the city council

3. who / good at / organize people

4. who / plan on / set up tables at the supermarkets

5. who / want / donate their services

6. who / like / help Erik practice for the debate

Who enjoys working with students?

Erik does.

Immigrants take the oath of allegiance to the United States during a citizenship ceremony at Liberty State Park in New Jersey.

A Discuss the questions.

1. Do you know anyone who has taken the naturalization test?
2. What do you think is the best way to prepare for the test?

READING NOTE

Multiple-Choice Test Strategies
1. Read the directions first. Ask the teacher or test examiner if you do not understand something.
2. Read each question carefully.
3. Read all of the answers. Try to eliminate wrong answers.
4. Select your answer. Fill in the circle next to your answer.
5. Watch the time. You may have to work more quickly depending on how much time you have left.

B **ACADEMIC** Read the naturalization test sample questions on the following page. Fill in the circle next to each correct answer.

C Check your answers below.

1. c 2. c 3. b 4. b 5. d 6. c 7. d 8. a 9. b 10. a 11. c

The Naturalization Test

1. What do the stars on the flag mean?
   - a. There is one star for each 100 citizens.
   - b. There is one star for each citizen.
   - **●** c. There is one star for each state.
   - d. There is one star for each president.

2. How many states are there in the United States?
   - a. 48
   - b. 49
   - c. 50
   - d. 51

3. When is Independence Day?
   - a. January 1st
   - b. July 4th
   - c. September 1st
   - d. November 25th

4. What do the thirteen stripes on the flag represent?
   - a. The first thirteen presidents
   - c. The first thirteen days of the country
   - b. The original thirteen colonies
   - d. Thirteen laws

5. From which country did the United States fight to win independence?
   - a. Germany
   - b. Ireland
   - c. France
   - d. Great Britain

6. Who was the first President of the United States?
   - a. Abraham Lincoln
   - c. George Washington
   - b. John Adams
   - d. Benjamin Franklin

7. Who becomes the President of the United States if the President dies?
   - a. the Secretary of State
   - c. the First Lady
   - b. the Secretary of Defense
   - d. the Vice President

8. Who makes the laws in the United States?
   - a. Congress
   - b. judges
   - c. the President
   - d. the governors

9. Which state borders Canada?
   - a. Tennessee
   - b. Montana
   - c. Arizona
   - d. North Carolina

10. Who was the President during the Great Depression and World War II?
    - a. Franklin D. Roosevelt
    - c. John F. Kennedy
    - b. Thomas Jefferson
    - d. Dwight D. Eisenhower

11. What movement tried to end racial discrimination?
    - a. the Boston Tea Party
    - c. the Civil Rights Movement
    - b. the Vietnam War protests
    - d. the Women's Suffrage Movement 🎧83

WRITING OUR STORIES | Political Platforms

A **CIVICS** The two candidates below are running for a position on the city council. Read their political platforms. Which person would you vote for? Why?

I believe in improving our community by attracting development to our city. I'm in favor of lowering taxes in order to bring in businesses such as the new paint factory. Our city must begin building the factory right away. We need new jobs for our citizens. I'm opposed to building a new library. We already have a library. A new library can wait, but jobs can't. In addition to creating jobs, I'm in favor of increasing parking meter fees to fifty cents per half hour. I manage a successful business, and the downtown areas need income to improve parking and the sidewalks. I have fifteen years of experience on the city council. You can count on me to serve you.

–Douglas McMurphy

It's time for a change. The citizens of this city are tired of hearing the same promises. They don't want to see more traffic, and they don't want to breathe factory pollution. They miss having peace and quiet in their neighborhoods. We don't need more development. Instead of building a paint factory, we should start building a new library. As a former high school teacher and member of the Board of Education, I believe a new library would be beneficial to everyone in the community. People could take free literacy classes there, and adults could take high school equivalency classes. In addition, I'm in favor of building more bicycle paths so that people can ride their bicycles more safely downtown. A vote for me is a vote for education in a more livable community.

–Angela Pierre

B **CIVICS** Imagine you're a candidate for the city council. In your notebook, write your political platform discussing two or three important issues in your community. In your platform, use the phrases below.

be in favor of	be opposed to	believe in
(Gerunds can be used after these phrases.)		

222 Unit 14

C **ACADEMIC** Circle *Fragment* or *Sentence*.

1.	After the airplane landed.	(Fragment)	Sentence
2.	He regrets not studying English before.	Fragment	Sentence
3.	When I considered leaving my country.	Fragment	Sentence
4.	Because I needed to learn English.	Fragment	Sentence
5.	I prefer to take the bus instead of driving myself.	Fragment	Sentence
6.	Is easy to learn English.	Fragment	Sentence

D **ACADEMIC** Check the political platform you wrote for sentence fragments.

E Exchange papers with a partner. Complete the sentences.

1. My partner is in favor of _____.

2. My partner is opposed to _____.

3. My partner believes in _____.

F **ACADEMIC** Find and correct the mistakes.

1. The mayor isn't planning on ~~run~~ running for another term.

2. The students know how giving presentations.

3. Because I haven't registered to vote yet.

4. I'm tired of walk in the snow.

5. My family encourages me study hard.

6. The city council is opposed building a new parking garage.

7. When I arrived in this country.

8. My daughter can't stand waits for the bus in cold weather.

CULTURE NOTE

To become a US citizen, you must show that you understand basic English.

During your naturalization test. . .

1. You must read one or more sentences and show that you understand the meaning.
2. You must write one of three sentences, and the testing officer must be able to read your writing.
3. You must answer questions about your application.
4. The testing officer will ask ten questions about US civics. You must answer six correctly.

A **CIVICS** Listen and write the questions. Then, match each question with the correct answer. 🎧84

_____f_____ **1.** What is the Bill of Rights? _____?

_____ **2.** _____?

_____ **3.** _____?

_____ **4.** _____?

_____ **5.** _____?

_____ **6.** _____?

_____ **7.** _____?

_____ **8.** _____?

a. the President

b. November

c. Washington, D.C.

d. four years

e. 18 years of age

f. the first ten amendments to the Constitution

g. freedom of speech

h. 100

B **CIVICS** **LET'S TALK.** Answer the questions in groups.

1. Who is the President of the United States? _____

2. Who is the Vice President of the United States? _____

3. Who is your state's Governor? _____

4. What is the capital of your state? _____

5. Who is one of your state senators? _____

C **CIVICS** Go online to find information on the naturalization process. Search "naturalization test" or "how to become a US citizen." Find and complete a practice test or practice exercises.

UNIT 1

Simple Present

Subject	Verb	
I You We They	study do not study don't study	English.
He She	studies does not study doesn't study	
It	works. does not work. doesn't work.	

STATEMENTS

Note:

The simple present can be used to describe everyday activities, habits, and repeated actions.

YES / NO QUESTIONS

Do / Does	Subject	Verb
Do	I you we they	work? study in the library? walk to school?
Does	he she	

SHORT ANSWERS

Affirmative	Negative
Yes, you **do**.	No, you **don't**.
Yes, I **do**.	No, I **don't**.
Yes, we **do**.	No, we **don't**.
Yes, they **do**.	No, they **don't**.
Yes, he **does**.	No, he **doesn't**.
Yes, she **does**.	No, she **doesn't**.

Note:

Use the auxiliaries *do* and *does* to form simple present questions. Do not change the main verb.

WH- QUESTIONS

Question Word	Do / Does	Subject	Verb
What Where When Why How How often	do	I you we they	study?
	does	he she	

WHO QUESTIONS

Who	Singular Verb
Who	**studies** English? **goes** to work? **lives** close to school?

Notes:

1. *Who* takes a singular verb when it asks about the subject. The answer may be singular or plural.

   Who **speaks** *English?*   *Joe* **does**.

   Who **goes** *to work?*   *Joe and Sara* **do**.

2. When *Who* asks about the object, the verb can be singular or plural depending on the subject of the question.

   Who **do** *you* **visit**?   *Who* **does** *she* **call**?

Present Continuous

STATEMENTS

Subject	Be	(not)	Verb + -ing
I	am		
You We They	are	(not)	using a computer. studying for a test. sitting at a desk.
He She	is		

Notes:

1. The present continuous is often used to talk about an action that is happening now.

   I **am using** a computer.

2. The present continuous can also describe a temporary action.

   He **is not working** at the moment.

   (Meaning: He plans to have a job in the future.)

YES / NO QUESTIONS

Be	Subject	Verb + -ing
Am	I	
Are	you we they	speaking English?
Is	he she	

SHORT ANSWERS

Affirmative	Negative
Yes, you **are**.	No, you **aren't**.
Yes, I **am**.	No, I'**m not**.
Yes, we **are**.	No, we **aren't**.
Yes, they **are**.	No, they **aren't**.
Yes, he **is**.	No, he **isn't**.
Yes, she **is**.	No, she **isn't**.

WH- QUESTIONS

Wh- Word	Be	Subject	Verb + -ing
	am	I	
What Where Why	are	you we they	studying? reading? writing?
	is	he she	

WHO QUESTIONS

Who	is	studying?

SHORT ANSWERS

I **am**.
You **are**.
We **are**.
Marta and Joe **are**.
Joe **is**.
Marta **is**.

NON-ACTION VERBS

appear	have	miss	smell
believe	hear	need	sound
belong	know	own	taste
feel	like	prefer	understand
hate	look	see	want

Notes:

1. Non-action verbs are usually used in the simple present, not the present continuous. Non-action verbs often show feelings, senses, thoughts, or possession.

   He **knows** my name.

   I **miss** my grandparents.

2. There are some exceptions, because some verbs can show both action and non-action.

   I'm **having** a cup of tea.

   How are you **feeling**?

   They're **seeing** a movie.

UNIT 2

Simple Past

STATEMENTS

I You We They He She It	moved didn't move	to the United States.

YES / NO QUESTIONS

Did	Subject	Verb
Did	I you we they he she	have any pets? live in the country? play sports?

WH- QUESTIONS

Wh- Word	Did	Subject	Verb
Where When How What time	did	I you we they he she	go to school?
How long		it	take?

SHORT ANSWERS

Yes, you **did**.	No, you **didn't**.
Yes, I **did**.	No, I **didn't**.
Yes, we **did**.	No, we **didn't**.
Yes, they **did**.	No, they **didn't**.
Yes, he **did**.	No, he **didn't**.
Yes, she **did**.	No, she **didn't**.

IRREGULAR VERBS

Base Form	Simple Past	Past Participle	Base Form	Simple Past	Past Participle
be	was / were	been	leave	left	left
bear	bore	born	lose	lost	lost
become	became	become	make	made	made
begin	began	begun	meet	met	met
break	broke	broken	pay	paid	paid
bring	brought	brought	put	put	put
buy	bought	bought	quit	quit	quit
catch	caught	caught	read	read	read
come	came	come	ride	rode	ridden
do	did	done	say	said	said
drink	drank	drunk	see	saw	seen
drive	drove	driven	sell	sold	sold
eat	ate	eaten	send	sent	sent
fall	fell	fallen	sit	sat	sat
feel	felt	felt	sleep	slept	slept
find	found	found	speak	spoke	spoken
forget	forgot	forgotten	spend	spent	spent
freeze	froze	frozen	steal	stole	stolen
get	got	got / gotten	take	took	taken
give	gave	given	teach	taught	taught
go	went	gone	tell	told	told
grow	grew	grown	think	thought	thought
have	had	had	throw	threw	thrown
hear	heard	heard	win	won	won
know	knew	known	write	wrote	written

Simple Past of *Be*

STATEMENTS		
I He She It	was was not wasn't	fast.
You We They	were were not weren't	young.

STATEMENTS WITH *THERE + BE*		
There	was	a garden.
	was not wasn't	a refrigerator.
	were	few schools.
	were not weren't	large schools.

YES / NO QUESTIONS		
Be	Subject	Place / Adjective
Was	I he she it	in the city? busy?
Were	you we they	

SHORT ANSWERS	
Affirmative	Negative
Yes, I **was**.	No, I **wasn't**.
Yes, he **was**.	No, he **wasn't**.
Yes, she **was**.	No, she **wasn't**.
Yes, it **was**.	No, it **wasn't**.
Yes, you **were**.	No, you **weren't**.
Yes, we **were**.	No, we **weren't**.
Yes, they **were**.	No, they **weren't**.

Past Continuous

STATEMENTS		
I He She	was was not wasn't	plant**ing** corn. driv**ing** a wagon. read**ing** to the children. cook**ing** dinner.
You We They	were were not weren't	

Note:

The past continuous can describe an action that was in progress at a specific time in the past.

They **were** cook**ing** dinner at 6 o'clock.

I **was** read**ing** to the children when I heard a noise.

YES / NO QUESTIONS		
Be	Subject	Verb
Was	I he she it	go**ing** to England?
Were	you we they	mov**ing**? plant**ing** vegetables?

WH- QUESTIONS			
Wh- Word	*Be*	Subject	Verb
What When Where Why	was	I he she it	eat**ing**? mov**ing**? cross**ing**?
	were	you we they	

USED TO		
Subject	*Used to*	Verb
I You We They He She	used to	**write** letters. **use** candles for light. **grow** vegetables.

Note:

Used to can be used to talk about a habit or a routine that you had in the past but that you don't have now.

I **used to drink** coffee. Now, I drink tea.

Who Questions in the Past

		QUESTIONS				ANSWERS
Simple Past	Subject	Who			called?	His mother called.
	Object	Who	did	he	call?	He called his brother.
Past Continuous	Subject	Who	was		waiting?	His brother was waiting.
	Object	Who	was	he	waiting for?	He was waiting for a friend.

UNIT 3

Future with *Be Going to*

STATEMENTS			
Subject	Be	Going to	Verb
I	am 'm am not 'm not	going to	move. change jobs. get married.
You We They	are 're are not 're not / aren't		
He She	is 's		
It	is not 's not / isn't		rain.

Notes:

1. We can use *be going to* to talk about future plans.

2. *Be going to* can also be used when you already know something will be true.

   It **is going to** rain.

   (Meaning: I heard the weather report.)

   We **are going to** have a test.

   (Meaning: The teacher announced the test.)

3. *Going to* is often pronounced *gonna* in speaking. Do not write *gonna*. Use the long form.

   It **is going to** be a difficult test.

YES / NO QUESTIONS			
Be	Subject	Going to	Verb
Am	I	going to	move? change jobs? go to college?
Are	you we they		
Is	he she		

SHORT ANSWERS	
Affirmative	Negative
Yes, you **are**.	No, you **aren't**.
Yes, I **am**.	No, I'**m not**.
Yes, we **are**.	No, we **aren't**.
Yes, they **are**.	No, they **aren't**.
Yes, he **is**.	No, he **isn't**.
Yes, she **is**.	No, she **isn't**.

WH- QUESTIONS				
Wh- Word	Be	Subject	Going to	Verb
What	are	you	going to	do?
How	are	we		get there?
Where	are	they		move?
Who	is	she		visit?
Who	is	—		help?
When	is	it		rain?

ANSWERS
I'm **going to** study.
We'**re going to** take the train.
They'**re going to** move to California.
She'**s going to visit** her cousins.
My teacher **is going to** help.
It'**s going to** rain tomorrow.

Present Continuous with Future Meaning

Note:

1. If a specific time in the future is stated or clear, the present continuous can express future time.

   I'm working tomorrow.   *He is leaving at 4:00.*

Future with *Will*

STATEMENTS		
Subject	*Will*	**Verb**
I You We They He She	will 'll	do it.
	will not won't	

Notes:

1. *Will* can be used to make an offer or a decision at the time of action.

   I will do it.

2. It is common to use the contraction *'ll.*

   I'll help you.

3. *Will* can also be used to make a promise.

   I will call you as soon as I arrive.

4. Both *will / won't* and *be (not) going to* can be used to make predictions.

   The United States will make new immigration laws.

   There are going to be more electric cars.

FUTURE TIME CLAUSES
<u>After I **study** hard for two years</u>, I'll graduate.   (time clause)   (main clause)
<u>When I **have** time</u>, I'm going to finish my degree.   (time clause)   (main clause)
I'll graduate <u>after I **study** hard for two years.</u> (main clause)   (time clause)
I'm going to finish my degree <u>when I **have** time.</u>   (main clause)   (time clause)

Notes:

1. Time clauses can begin with words such as *after, before,* or *when.*

2. Use a comma when the time clause is at the beginning of a sentence.

3. Do not use a comma when the time clause is at the end of a sentence.

4. Use the simple present in the time clause. Use a future form in the main clause.

UNIT 4

Must / Must not

STATEMENTS		
Subject	*Must*	**Verb**
I You We They He She	must	stop at a red light. drive under the speed limit.
	must not	drive without a license.

Notes:

1. We can use *must* to describe rules, obligation, or necessity.

   *Drivers **must stop** at stop signs.*

2. We can use *must not* to describe an action that is not permitted.

   *You **must not drive** through a red light.*

3. *Must* in the question form is very formal and is rarely used.

   ***Must** I **pay** my ticket?*

Have to / Doesn't have to / Don't have to

STATEMENTS		
Subject	*Have to*	Verb
I	have to	wear a seatbelt.
You We They	do not have to don't have to	buy a new car.
He She	has to	drive with a license.
	does not have to doesn't have to	wash the car.

YES / NO QUESTIONS			
Do / Does	Subject	*Have to*	Verb
Do	you we they	have to	do laundry? buy stamps? see the dentist?
Does	he she		

Notes:

1. *Have to* can describe necessity or obligation.

   I **have to get** car insurance.

2. *Have to* can substitute for *must*.

   You **must stop** at a red light.

   You **have to stop** at a red light.

3. *Doesn't have to / Don't have to* can describe something that is not necessary.

   You **don't have to own** a car in New York City.

4. Do not confuse *don't have to* with *must not*.

   I **must not drive** at night.

   (Meaning: It is against the law.)

   I **don't have to drive** at night.

   (Meaning: It is not necessary because I work in the morning.)

Can / Can't

STATEMENTS		
Subject	*Can*	Verb
I You We They He She	can	drive. park here.
	cannot can't	

YES / NO QUESTIONS		
Can	Subject	Verb
Can	I you we they he she	drive a truck? swim? speak French?

Notes:

1. We can use *can* to describe ability. We can use *can't / cannot* to describe inability.

   I **can** drive a car, but I **can't** drive a truck.

2. We can also use *can* to describe a permitted action. We can use *cannot / can't* to describe an action that is not permitted.

   I **can drive** at night by myself.

   You **can't drive** through red lights.

Could / Couldn't

STATEMENTS		
Subject	*Could*	Verb
I You We They He She	could	speak English. find a job. drive a car.
	could not couldn't	

YES / NO QUESTIONS		
Could	Subject	Verb
Could	I you we they he she	speak English? find a job? drive a car?

Note:

We can use *could* to describe past ability. We can use *could not / couldn't* to describe past inability.

   I **could** drive when I came to this country.

   I **couldn't** speak English when I came here.

Should / Should not

STATEMENTS		
Subject	*Should*	Verb
I You We They He She	should	**drive** carefully. **buy** a new car.
	should not shouldn't	**drive** at night. **park** there.

Notes:

1. We can use *should* to express an opinion or give advice.

   I **should buy** a smaller car. Small cars get good gas mileage.

2. We can use *should not / shouldn't* to show that something is not a good idea.

   You **shouldn't park** there. There is not enough space.

Had better / Had better not

STATEMENTS		
Subject	*Had better*	Verb
I You We They He She	had better 'd better	**wear** a seat belt. **use** a car seat.
	had better not 'd better not	**drive** without a license. **forget** to fill the gas tank.

Note:

Had better / Had better not can express warnings. *Had better / Had better not* are stronger than *should / should not*.

> You**'d better check** your tire.
> (Or you'll get a flat tire.)

> I**'d better not miss** another class.
> (Or I'll fail the class.)

UNIT 5

Yes / No Questions Review

SIMPLE PRESENT		
Do	I you we they	cook?
Does	he she	

PRESENT CONTINUOUS		
Am	I	
Are	you we they	cooking?
Is	he she	

SIMPLE PAST		
Did	I you we they he she	cook?

SIMPLE PAST OF *BE*		
Was	I he she	busy?
Were	you we they	

FUTURE WITH *BE GOING TO*			
Am	I		
Are	you we they	going to	cook?
Is	he she		

FUTURE WITH *WILL*		
Will	I you we they he she	cook?

QUESTIONS WITH *WHO* AND *WHOSE*

Whose umbrella is that?	It's mine.
Who likes sports?	I do.
Who do you play cards with?	I play with my cousins.

Notes:

1. *Whose* asks questions about possession.
2. *Who* asks questions about the subject or object.

Who Questions: Present and Past

PRESENT		
Subject	Who **goes** to the gym every day?	<u>Beth</u> does.
Object	Who **does** Beth **go** to the gym with?	She goes <u>with her sister</u>.

PAST		
Subject	Who **went** to the gym?	<u>Jim</u> did.
Object	Who **did** Jim **go** to the gym with?	He went <u>with his wife</u>.

QUESTIONS WITH *HOW*

How do you get to work?	I take <u>the bus</u>.
How far do you live from school?	I live about <u>three miles</u> away.
How long did you wait?	I waited <u>30 minutes</u>.
How much money do you have?	I have <u>$4.00</u>.
How many tickets do you have?	I only have <u>two</u>.
How often do you come to school?	I come to school <u>three days a week</u>.

TAG QUESTIONS

Simple Present of *be*	You **are** from Thailand,	**aren't** you?
	It **isn't** cold today,	**is** it?
Present continuous	They **are having** a nice time,	**aren't** they?
	They **aren't having** a bad time,	**are** they?
Simple present	He **plays** soccer every day,	**doesn't** he?
	He **doesn't play** tennis,	**does** he?
Simple Past of *be*	They **were** at the park,	**weren't** they?
	They **weren't** at home,	**were** they?
Simple past	You **took** some pictures,	**didn't** you?
	You **didn't take** these pictures,	**did** you?
Future with *will*	She **will plant** more roses,	**won't** she?
	She **won't plant** any vegetables,	**will** she?

UNIT 6

May and Might for Possibilities

SIMPLE PRESENT STATEMENTS		
Subject	May / Might	Verb
I You We They He She	may might may not might not	go on vacation. need a visa.

Note:

May (not) or *might (not)* can be used to express possibilities.

I **might go** on vacation.

(Meaning: Maybe I will go on vacation.)

He **may not need** a visa.

(Meaning: Maybe he doesn't need a visa.)

PRESENT CONTINUOUS STATEMENTS			
Subject	May / Might	Be	Verb + -ing
I You We They He She	might may	be	arriving late. driving.

Note:

The present continuous form of *might* and *may* can be used to describe actions possibly occurring now or in the near future.

A: *Where are they going?*

B: *They* **might be going** *to Europe.*

Must for Inferences

STATEMENTS		
Subject	Must	Verb
I You We They He She	must	have the flu. speak French.

Notes:

1. *Must* can be used to make an inference. An inference is a guess about something that seems true.

   Situation: *Ann is walking outside in the winter. The temperature is 20° F, and Ann is wearing a T-shirt.*

   Inference: *Ann* **must be** *cold.*

2. *Must* can also be used to express empathy (show that you understand another person's feelings).

   You **must be** *tired.*

Could for Suggestions

STATEMENTS		
Subject	Could	Verb
You We They He She	could	buy tickets online. bring a backpack.

Note:

Could can be used to make suggestions.

A: *How should I get to the airport?*

B: *You* **could take** *the shuttle.*

Would Rather and Would Prefer to

YES / NO QUESTIONS				ANSWERS			
Would	Subject	Prefer to / Rather	Verb	Subject	Would	Prefer to / Rather	Verb
Would	I you we they he she	prefer to rather	drive?	I You We They He She	would 'd	prefer to rather	fly.

Notes:

1. *Would rather* and *would prefer to* can be used to express preferences.

   I **would rather go** to New York than Miami.

   I **would prefer to go** to Chicago rather than Dallas.

2. The contractions are *'d rather* or *'d prefer to*.

   He**'d rather fly**.

   They**'d prefer to drive**.

UNIT 7

Present Perfect Continuous

STATEMENTS			
Subject	Have	Been	Verb + -ing
I You We They	have 've	been	playing tennis for two hours.
He She	has 's		

Notes:

1. The present continuous can be used to describe an action that is happening now.

   I **am playing** tennis.

2. We can use the present perfect continuous to describe an action that began in the past and is continuing now or has recently ended.

   I **have been swimming** for an hour.

For and Since

Notes:

1. *For* shows an amount of time.

   I've been watching the game **for** a few minutes.

   He's been training **for** three days.

2. *Since* shows when an action started.

   I've been watching the game **since** 5:00.

   He's been training **since** Monday.

YES / NO QUESTIONS

Have / Has	Subject	Been	Verb + -ing
Have	I you we they	been	watching the game? playing with a team? working hard?
Has	he she		

SHORT ANSWERS

Affirmative	Negative
Yes, you have. Yes, I have. Yes, we have. Yes, they have. Yes, he has. Yes, she has.	No, you haven't. No, I haven't. No, we haven't. No, they haven't. No, he hasn't. No, she hasn't.

HOW LONG QUESTIONS

How long	Have	Subject	Been	Verb + -ing
How long	have	I you we they	been	studying English? living here?
	has	he she		

Note:

How long can be used to ask about length of time.

I've been studying English <u>for two months</u>.

He's been living here <u>since 2017</u>.

UNIT 8

Present Perfect Simple

STATEMENTS WITH *FOR* / *SINCE*

I You We They	have 've have not haven't		
He She	has 's has not hasn't	worked there	for two years. since January. since the company opened.

Notes:

1. To form the present perfect simple, use *have / has* and the past participle.

2. The present perfect simple can be used to describe an action that began in the past and is still true in the present.

   *They **have lived** in the city **for** many years.*   *She **hasn't seen** him **since** they broke up.*

3. The present perfect simple can also be used to describe changes.

   *He **has lost** over 50 pounds **since** he started exercising.*   *In the past year, Lily **has grown** three inches.*

Past Participles

See page 227 for the irregular verb chart.

Present Perfect Simple for the Recent Past

Notes:

1. Use the present perfect simple with words such as *just, lately,* and *recently* to describe an action in the recent past.

2. Put *just* between *have / has* and the main verb.

   *I **have just quit** my job.*

3. *Lately* is often placed at the end of a sentence.

   *He **hasn't been** in class **lately**.*

4. *Recently* is often placed between *have / has* and the main verb, or at the end of the sentence.

   *They **have recently become** grandparents.*

   *They **have become** grandparents **recently**.*

Already and Yet

Notes:

1. *Already* can show that an action is completed. *Already* is often used in affirmative sentences. You can use the present perfect simple or the simple past with *already*. The simple past is more often used with *already* in spoken English than in writing.

   She has **already bought** the invitations.   She **already bought** the invitations.

2. *Already* is usually placed between *have / has* and the main verb, or at the end of the sentence.

   She **has already bought** the invitations.   She **has bought** the invitations **already**.

3. *Yet* can show that an action has not been completed. *Yet* is often used at the end of questions and negative sentences. You can use the present perfect simple or the simple past with *yet*.

   Has she **sent** the invitations **yet**?   **Did** she **send** the invitations **yet**?

   She **hasn't sent** the invitations **yet**.   She **didn't send** the invitations **yet**.

Contrast: Present Perfect Simple, Present Perfect Continuous, and Simple Past

Notes:

1. The present perfect simple can be used to describe actions that began in the past and are true in the present. The present perfect simple can also describe events in the recent past.

   I **have been** in this country for three years.   They **have just won** the lottery.

2. The present perfect continuous can be used to describe actions that began in the past and are continuing now or have recently ended.

   We **have been working** at the restaurant since we moved here.

3. The simple past can be used to describe actions that were completed in the past.

   She **graduated** from college in 2016.   They **moved** to New Mexico two years ago.

UNIT 9

How long and *How many*

Notes:

1. *How long* can ask about an amount of time. *How long* can be used with the present perfect continuous.

   A: **How long** has she been repairing the TV?

   B: She has been repairing it **for an hour**.

2. *How many* asks about a specific number. *How many* can be used with the present perfect simple.

   A: **How many TVs** has she repaired this week?

   B: She has repaired **three TVs** so far.

Present Perfect Simple for Repeated Actions

Notes:

1. The present perfect simple can be used to describe repeated past actions.

2. The following time expressions often signal a repeated action:

   from time to time   I have been late **from time to time**.

   a few times   She has worked overtime **a few times**.

Ever and *Never*

Notes:

1. *Ever* and *never* are often used with the present perfect simple. *Ever* means *at any time* and is often used in *Yes / No* questions or when comparing things.

   *Have you **ever** been to France?*

   *This is the best job I've **ever** had.*

2. *Never* means *not at any time*. It is often used in statements, but it can't be used with a negative verb.

   *I have **never** worked at a school.*

Present Perfect Simple: Word Order

1. Time expressions are usually placed at the end of a sentence.

   *I have worked here **since 2005**.*   *I have changed jobs **twice**.*

   *I have worked here **for two years**.*   *She's taken four breaks **so far**!*

2. Adverbs of frequency are often placed before the main verb in a sentence.

   *Laura has **never** received a warning at work.*   *She has **always** been an excellent employee.*

3. *Just* and *finally* are usually placed before the main verb in a sentence.

   *Henry has **just** gotten a raise.*   *Andrea has **finally** finished her project.*

4. *Already* is placed before the main verb or at the end of the sentence.

   *They have **already** repaired three computers.*   *They have repaired three computers **already**.*

5. *Yet* and *recently* are usually placed at the end of the sentence. *Yet* is usually used in questions and negative sentences.

   *I've spoken to him **recently**.*   *Bill hasn't spoken to the supervisor **yet**.*

Contrast: Present Perfect Simple and Present Perfect Continuous

Notes:

1. Some verbs can be used in either the present perfect simple or the present perfect continuous. When used in the present perfect simple, the verb shows the **result** of an action. When used in the present perfect continuous, the verb shows the **duration** or **continuation** of an action.

   *They **have worked** very hard on this project.*

   *They **have been working** on this project since last month.*

2. Other verbs, especially non-action verbs, can be used in the present perfect simple but not the present perfect continuous.

   *Jake **has needed** some help with his homework recently.*

   *I **have owned** this car for ten years.*

3. There are some exceptions to this rule. Some verbs can show both action and non-action.

   *Maria **has been having** a good experience at this company.*

Contrast: Simple Past and Present Perfect Simple

Notes:

1. The simple past is often used to describe an action that happened at a specific time in the past. The action is complete.

   *I **finished** my deliveries <u>an hour ago</u>.*

   *We **had to work** overtime <u>from 5:00 to 8:00</u>.*

2. The present perfect simple is often used to describe an action that happened in the recent past and is still true now. This action may continue in the future.

   *They'**ve** already **used** this equipment.*

   *I'**ve applied** to that company twice, and I may apply again.*

UNIT 10

Should have for Regrets and Expectations

STATEMENTS

I You We They He She	should have should not have shouldn't have	**brought** food. **opened** the box.

Notes:

1. The past modal is formed with the modal + *have* + the past participle.

2. *Should have* can be used to express regret about a past action.

   *I **should have studied** more.*

   (Meaning: I didn't study enough.)

   *They **shouldn't have left** their umbrellas at home.*

   (Meaning: It rained; they weren't prepared.)

3. *Should have / Shouldn't have* can also be used to describe expectations about the past that were not met.

   *The bus **should have arrived** by now.*   *I **shouldn't have gotten** a D on this exam.*

   (Meaning: The bus is late.)   (Meaning: My grade is lower than expected.)

May have, Might have, and *Could have* for Past Possibilities

STATEMENTS

Subject	*May / Might / Could + Have*	Past Participle
I You We They He She	may have might have could have may not have might not have	**gone** to the movies. **forgotten** to bring it. **bought** a new car.

Notes:

1. *May (not) have, might (not) have,* and *could have* can be used to express past possibilities.

   *They **may have taken** it.* (Meaning: Maybe they took it.)

   *She **might not have remembered** it.* (Meaning: Maybe she forgot it.)

2. *Could not have (Couldn't have)* can be used to express past impossibilities.

   *You **couldn't have been** at work that day. You were in the emergency room with your daughter.*

Must have for Inferences

STATEMENTS		
Subject	*Must + Have*	Past Participle
I You We They He She	must have must not have	left his keys at home. remembered them.

Notes:

1. *Must (not) have* can be used to express an inference about a past action.

   Situation: *I don't have my keys with me. I left the house this morning, and I think the keys were on the kitchen table. I don't remember locking the door.*

   Inferences: *I **must have left** my keys at home.*

       *I **must not have remembered** to bring my keys.*

2. *Must have* can also be used to express empathy about the past. When used with adjectives, the form is usually *must have* + past participle of *be* + adjective.

   A: *I failed my driver's test.*

   B: *You **must have been** disappointed.*

UNIT 11

Simple Present Passive

STATEMENTS			
Subject	*Be*	Past Participle	
Cotton	is	grown	in Texas.
	is not		in Washington.
Computer chips	are	manufactured	in New Mexico.
	are not		in Oklahoma.

Notes:

1. **Active** sentences usually emphasize the person or thing that does the action.

   *Fishermen **catch** salmon in Washington.*

2. **Passive** sentences usually emphasize the person or thing that receives the action.

   *Salmon **are caught** in Washington.*

YES / NO QUESTIONS		
Is	milk	produced in Wisconsin?
Are	tires	manufactured in Ohio?

SHORT ANSWERS	
Yes, it **is**.	No, it **isn't**.
Yes, they **are**.	No, they **aren't**.

WH- QUESTIONS			
Where	is	rice	grown?
How	are	cars	manufactured?

ANSWERS

Rice **is grown** in many Asian countries.
Cars **are manufactured** on assembly lines in factories.

Count and Non-Count Nouns

Notes:

1. A count noun requires either a singular or plural verb.

   *This apple **is** delicious.*

   *Apples **are** grown in Washington State.*

2. A non-count noun requires a singular verb.

   *Lettuce **is** grown in Arizona.*

Simple Present Passive with *By*

Notes:

1. In passive sentences, include the person or thing that does the action when it is important and not obvious. Use *by*.

   *This candy **is produced by Royal Sweets**.*   *This toy **is made by an American company**.*

2. Don't use *by* if the person or thing that does the action is obvious, unimportant, or unknown.

   *This chocolate **is made** in Switzerland.*   (*By* is not necessary because we know that a candy company makes the candy.)

   *Cows **are raised** on farms.*   (*By* is not necessary because it is obvious that farmers raise the cows.)

UNIT 12

Simple Past Passive

STATEMENTS			
Subject	*Be*	Past Participle	
The insulin pump	was	invented	by Dean Kamen.
	was not		last year.
747 jumbo jets	were	designed	by Boeing engineers.
	were not		in the 1800s.

ACTIVE VS. PASSIVE	
Active	NASA **invented** the space shuttle.
Passive	The space shuttle **was invented** by NASA.

Notes:

1. **Active** sentences usually emphasize the person or thing that does the action.

2. **Passive** sentences usually emphasize the person or thing that receives the action.

Simple Past Passive with *By*

Notes:

1. In past passive sentences, include the person or thing that did the action when it is important and not obvious. Use *by*.

   *The hepatitis B vaccine **was invented by Baruch Blumberg**.*

2. When the person or thing that did the action is obvious, unimportant, or unknown, it does not need to be included.

   *Many years ago, medical equipment **was not sterilized**.*

OTHER PASSIVE FORMS	
Simple present	Airbags **are installed** in all cars.
Present continuous	Those cars **are being repaired**.
Simple past	Airbags **were installed** in 1973.
Past continuous	My car **was being repaired** while I was waiting.
Future with *will*	A new model **will be delivered** tomorrow.
Future with *be going to*	That car **is going to be inspected** tomorrow.
Present perfect simple	Many improvements **have been made** to today's cars.

Note:

All passive verbs use a form of the verb *to be* + the past participle.

UNIT 13

Relative Clauses with *Who, Which, Whom,* and *Whose*

Notes:

1. A relative clause describes or gives more information about a noun. Relative clauses can begin with relative pronouns such as *who, which, whom,* and *whose*.

   Who introduces information about a person.

   <u>My father</u>, **who used to play in a band**, is now a high school music teacher.

   Which introduces information about a place or thing.

   The music for <u>West Side Story</u>, **which was both a Broadway musical and a movie**, was written by Leonard Bernstein.

   Whom introduces information about a person; this person must be the object of the relative clause.

   She's writing a song for her son. She named <u>her son</u> after her father.

   She's writing a song for <u>her son</u>, **whom she named after her father**.

   Whose acts as a possessive form in the relative clause; a noun always follows *whose*.

   John Lennon is still famous today. <u>His</u> wife and sons also have musical talent.

   John Lennon, **whose wife and sons also have musical talent**, is still famous today.

Relative Clauses with *That*

Notes:

1. There are two types of relative clauses: **non-restrictive** and **restrictive**. A non-restrictive clause gives extra information about a noun. Commas are used to separate a non-restrictive clause from a main clause. *Which* is only used with non-restrictive clauses.

   We paid <u>Dave Jones</u>, **whom we hired to sing at our wedding**.

   (Meaning: We know who Dave Jones is. The relative clause gives extra information about Dave Jones.)

   <u>Radio City Music Hall</u>, **which was opened in 1932**, can hold 6,015 people.

   (Meaning: We know Radio City Music Hall. The relative clause gives extra information about it.)

2. A restrictive clause gives essential information about the noun it describes. Commas are *not* used with restrictive clauses.

   <u>The students</u> **who studied at Juilliard** were great musicians.

   (Meaning: We do not know who the students are without the clause. The clause is necessary.)

3. The relative pronoun *that* can be used in restrictive clauses to replace *who* or *whom* in casual speech. This is not acceptable in academic writing.

   <u>The man</u> **that we hired to sing at our wedding** was very talented.

Relative Clauses with *When* and *Where*

Notes:

1. Relative clauses can also begin with *when* and *where*.

   When introduces information about a time.

   Where introduces information about a place.

2. Both *when* and *where* can be used with non-restrictive and restrictive clauses.

   Carnegie Hall is located in <u>Midtown Manhattan</u>, **where it was built in 1890**.

   It opened in <u>an era</u> **when the neighborhood was not used to such a large building**.

UNIT 14

Verb + Infinitive

Notes:

1. When two verbs are used together, the second verb is often an infinitive. An infinitive is *to* + the base form of the verb.

   *I **plan to become** a US citizen.*

   *Luciana **prepared to take** the naturalization test.*

2. We can use an infinitive after the following verbs:

afford	fail	like	prefer	try
agree	forget	love	prepare	volunteer
ask	hate	manage	promise	wait
be able	hope	need	refuse	want
choose	intend	offer	remember	wish
decide	know how	plan	seem	would like
expect	learn (how)			

Verb + Object + Infinitive

Notes:

1. An object or object pronoun + an infinitive can be used after the following verbs:

advise	encourage	hire	remind	urge
allow	expect	invite	require	want
ask	forbid	permit	teach	warn
convince	help	persuade	tell	

   *My supervisor **expects me to use** English with all of the customers.*

   *Her parents **have encouraged her to learn** both English and Spanish.*

2. For negative sentences, place *not* before the infinitive.

   *The interviewer **reminded us not to arrive** late to the ceremony.*

Be + Adjective + Infinitive

Note:

1. The infinitive form can be used after the following adjectives:

dangerous	good	important	polite	selfish
difficult	hard	impossible	possible	stressful
easy	healthy	interesting	reasonable	terrible
expensive	helpful	necessary	romantic	wonderful

   *It's **stressful to move** to a new country.*

   *It was **helpful to have** a study partner.*

Verb + Gerund

Notes:

1. When two verbs are used together, the second verb can also be a gerund. A gerund is a verb + *ing*. Gerunds can be used after the following verbs:

admit	can't help	discuss	miss	recall
anticipate	can't stand	enjoy	postpone	recommend
appreciate	consider	imagine	practice	regret
avoid	delay	mind	quit	stop

   They **missed** <u>*seeing*</u> *their family during the holiday season.*

2. For negative sentences, put *not* before the gerund.

   *She **regretted** <u>not</u> **working** with people who spoke English.*

Preposition + Gerund

Notes:

1. Gerunds can be used in time clauses with *after*, *before*, or *while* if the subject is the same in both the time clause and the main clause.

   After Maria studied *for the naturalization test, she passed easily.*

   After <u>*studying*</u> *for the naturalization test, Maria passed easily.*

   I studied for my English exam, ***while I was waiting*** *for my interview.*

   I studied for my English exam ***while*** <u>*waiting*</u> *for my interview.*

2. A gerund can also be used after *in addition to*, *instead of*, or *without*.

   Many immigrants take a citizenship class ***in addition to*** <u>*working*</u>*.*

Note:

1. Gerunds can be used after the following verb + preposition phrases:

adjust to	dream about	think about
believe in	look forward to	tire of
care about	plan on	worry about
complain about	talk about	

   *When Paul lived in Poland, he **dreamed about** <u>moving</u> to the United States.*

Contrast: Infinitives and Gerunds

*It was **impossible** <u>to find</u> a job in my country.*

*My friends **didn't encourage me** <u>to speak</u> English.*

*He **enjoyed** <u>working</u> at the real estate office.*

After <u>working</u> for a few years at a factory, I found another job.

Present Continuous Verbs

1. For most verbs, add *-ing*.
   walk – walking   play – playing   eat – eating

2. If a verb ends in *e*, drop the *e* and add *-ing*.
   write – writing   come – coming   drive – driving

3. If a verb ends in a consonant + vowel + consonant, double the final consonant and add *-ing*.
   sit – sitting   run – running   put – putting

Simple Present Verbs: Third Person

1. For most verbs, add *-s*.
   make – makes   call – calls   sleep – sleeps

2. If a verb ends with a consonant + *y*, change the *y* to *i* and add *-es*.
   try – tries   cry – cries   apply – applies

3. If a verb ends with *sh, ch, x, s*, or *z*, add *-es*.
   wash – washes   watch – watches   fix – fixes

4. These verbs are irregular in the third person.
   have – has   do – does   go – goes

Simple Past Verbs

1. For most verbs, add *-d* or *-ed*.
   rent – rented   save – saved

2. If a verb ends in a consonant + vowel + consonant, double the final consonant and add *-ed*.
   stop – stopped   rob – robbed

3. If a verb ends in *w, x*, or *y*, do not double the consonant. Add *-ed*.
   play – played   relax – relaxed   snow – snowed

4. If a verb ends in a consonant + *y*, change the *y* to *i* and add *-ed*.
   try – tried   study – studied

Comparative Adjectives: *-er*

1. For most adjectives, add *-r* or *-er*.
   cold – colder   wide – wider   tall – taller

2. If a one-syllable adjective ends in a consonant + vowel + consonant, double the final consonant and add *-er*.
   big – bigger   thin – thinner   sad – sadder

3. If an adjective ends in a consonant + *y*, change the *y* to *i* and add *-er*.
   happy – happier   heavy – heavier   friendly – friendlier

Superlative Adjectives: *-est*

1. For most adjectives, add *-st* or *-est*.
   large – largest   short – shortest   tall – tallest

2. If a one-syllable adjective ends in a consonant + vowel + consonant, double the final consonant and add *-est*.
   big – biggest   thin – thinnest   sad – saddest

3. If an adjective ends in a consonant + *y*, change the *y* to *i* and add *-est*.
   busy – busiest   noisy – noisiest   friendly – friendliest

UNIT 5

Student 1: Read the questions in Set A to Student 2. Then, listen to Student 2 and write the questions.

Student 2: Read the questions in Set B to Student 1.

Set A
1. Who taught you how to cook?
2. What kind of cooking classes did you take?
3. Do you watch cooking shows on TV?
4. Is your kitchen big enough for you?
5. What are you going to cook for dinner tonight?

Set B
6. Does your husband like to cook?
7. What classes did you take together?
8. What was the first dish that you cooked?
9. Who is going to cook dinner at your house tonight?
10. Why did you decide to go to cooking school?

UNIT 6

Student 1: Read Set A sentences to Student 2. Then, listen to Student 2 and write each sentence next to the correct picture.

Student 2: Read Set B sentences to Student 1.

Set A
a. They might retire soon.
b. They may not go to college right away.
c. They could take their honeymoon later.
d. They may look for full-time jobs.
e. They would rather rent an apartment first.
f. They would prefer to be closer to their grandchildren.

Set B
a. They could move in with their children.
b. They'd prefer to buy a house in a few years.
c. They may not work at the same place.
d. They might wait to have children.
e. They would rather study part time.
f. They may volunteer at the library.

UNIT 7

Student 1: Read Set A sentences to Student 2. Then, listen to Student 2 and write each sentence next to the correct picture.

Student 2: Read Set B sentences to Student 1.

Set A
a. You haven't been coming to work on time.
b. It's been making a strange noise.
c. My stomach has been bothering me.
d. It's been leaking oil.
e. We've been receiving a lot of complaints.
f. They've been running for two hours.
g. I've been feeling very tired.
h. They've been drinking a lot of water.

Set B
a. It's been overheating in traffic.
b. I've been having trouble sleeping.
c. The crowd has been cheering for them.
d. You've been making mistakes in your work.
e. Roger has been in the lead for 30 minutes.
f. It hasn't been running smoothly.
g. You've been arguing with your coworkers.
h. I haven't been eating well.

UNIT 9

Student 1: Read Set A questions to Student 2. Then, listen to Student 2 and answer the questions about the pictures in complete sentences. Use the words in the boxes and the simple past or present perfect simple.

Student 2: Read Set B questions to Student 1.

Set A

1. How many employees has she fired this year?
2. How long has he been working at this garage?
3. What time did he start work this morning?
4. How many doctors did she talk to this morning?
5. How long has she been selling homes?
6. How long has he had his own business?

Set B

1. How many employees did she hire?
2. How many cars has he repaired today?
3. How many streets has he cleared so far?
4. How many patients has she helped today?
5. How many homes did she sell this month?
6. How many systems has he installed today?

UNIT 10

Student 1: Listen to Student 2 talk about last weekend. Be a good listener and give an appropriate response. Use *must have been* and an adjective from the box. Then, switch roles and read sentences 6-10 to Student 2.

Student 2: Listen to Student 1 talk about last weekend. Be a good listener and give an appropriate response. Use *must have been* and an adjective from the box.

disappointed	pleased	surprised
excited	proud	thrilled
exhausted	scared	worried
frustrated		

My homework was very difficult.

You must have been frustrated.

APPENDIX D / Dictation

UNIT 1

1. Are any students eating?
2. Are all the students writing in their notebooks?
3. Does anyone have a pencil sharpener?
4. Do you go to work after class?
5. Who is sitting next to you?
6. How many hours a week do you study for this class?

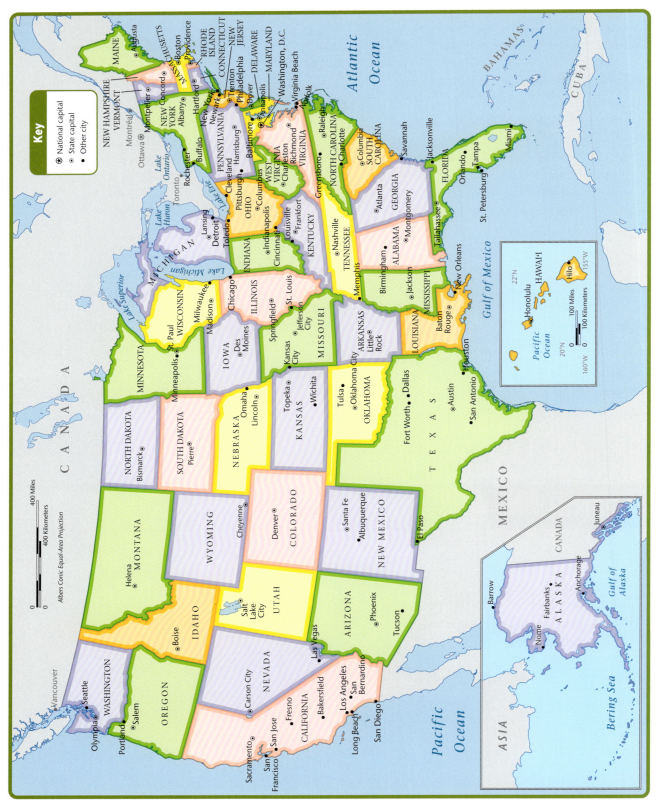

US Map